Ella Kovács (Szabó), age 18, high school graduation ball,
Hódmezővásárhely, Hungary, 1948.

Elegant Hungarian Tortes and Homestyle Desserts for American Bakers

Ella Kovács Szabó
with Eve Aino Roza Wirth

Edited and with additional material
by Sharon Hudgins

Number 6 in the Great American Cooking Series

University of North Texas Press
Denton, Texas

10 9 8 7 6 5 4 3 2 1

Permissions:
University of North Texas Press
1155 Union Circle #311336
Denton, TX 76203-5017

The paper used in this book meets the minimum requirements of the American National Standard for Permanence of Paper for Printed Library Materials, z39.48.1984. Binding materials have been chosen for durability.

Library of Congress Cataloging-in-Publication Data

Names: Szabó, Ella Kovács, 1929-2009, author. | Wirth, Eve Aino Roza, 1966- author. | Hudgins, Sharon, editor, writer of preface, writer of added commentary.
Title: Elegant Hungarian tortes and homestyle desserts for American bakers / Ella Kovács Szabó with Eve Aino Roza Wirth; edited and with additional material by Sharon Hudgins.
Other titles: Great American cooking series; no. 6.
Description: Denton : University of North Texas Press, [2023] | Series: Number 6 in the Great American Cooking Series | Includes bibliographical references and index.
Identifiers: LCCN 2023044072 (print) | LCCN 2023044073 (ebook) | ISBN 9781574419146 (cloth) | ISBN 9781574419252 (ebook)
Subjects: LCSH: Cooking, Hungarian. | Desserts--Hungary. | Cake--Hungary. | Baking--United States. | BISAC: COOKING / Courses & Dishes / Desserts | COOKING / Regional & Ethnic / American / Southwestern States | LCGFT: Cookbooks.
Classification: LCC TX723.5.H8 S88 2023 (print) | LCC TX723.5.H8 (ebook) | DDC 641.86/09439--dc23/eng/20231017
LC record available at https://lccn.loc.gov/2023044072
LC ebook record available at https://lccn.loc.gov/2023044073

Elegant Hungarian Tortes and Homestyle Desserts for American Bakers is Number 6 in the Great American Cooking Series.

The electronic edition of this book was made possible by the support of the Vick Family Foundation.

Typeset by vPrompt eServices.

CONTENTS

PART ONE:
NUT-FLOUR TORTES AND ROULADES

PART TWO:
HUNGARIAN HOMESTYLE DESSERTS

EDITOR'S PREFACE

The story of how this cookbook came to be published is truly remarkable—a set of improbable circumstances that led to the book you are holding in your hands today. In the pages following this preface, you'll read Ella Szabó's own account of how these recipes survived a war in Europe and ultimately came into her possession in America.

I first met Ella Szabó around 2006 on a monthly Teleforum organized by the International Association of Culinary Professionals, of which both of us were members. Teleforums, or teleconferences, were the forerunner of today's Zoom meetings, where people from all over the world gathered on a group telephone call to discuss a particular topic. The subject that day was "Publishing Your Cookbook with a University Press," and the key speaker was Ron Chrisman, director of the University of North Texas Press (UNTP), which had recently begun publishing a series of cookbooks by American authors. As an author who already had two books published by university presses and was currently under contract to UNTP for a cookbook myself, I was the secondary speaker.

A few days later, Ella phoned me to seek my advice about a cookbook project she was working on and to ask more about the publishing process. I was intrigued by her story of family recipes lost in Europe during World War II, then miraculously recovered after the war, and how they eventually made their way to the United States and into her hands, igniting her passion for baking. I asked her to send me that story and a few sample recipes, which I offered to read and comment on.

When her package arrived in the mail, I realized that the story of the lost-and-found recipes, her own experiences as a baker and caterer, and the recipes themselves had the makings of a good book. Its focus was on Central European, especially Hungarian, nut-flour tortes like those served in the pastry shops and coffeehouses of Budapest and Vienna, and she included a selection of traditional Hungarian homestyle desserts, too.

Having traveled extensively in Hungary myself—and eaten at many of the coffeehouses and pastry shops she described—I knew that her recipes were authentic. The majority of them were made with nut flours, not wheat flour, which meant they were also gluten free. Her book was especially timely, because "gluten free" had just become the latest health-food fad in America. More important, though, I knew that avoiding gluten was necessary for people with genuine wheat allergies and especially for people with the serious autoimmune condition celiac disease. Most of Ella's recipes would make delicious desserts not only for home cooks in general but also for those people with dietary restrictions against gluten.

I encouraged Ella to finish the manuscript and send it back to me for editorial comments before submitting it to a publisher. But I never heard from her again. I just assumed that other projects of hers had taken precedence or that her life had taken a different turn, which, sadly, it had.

In 2012 the managing editor of UNTP sent me a cookbook manuscript to read and evaluate. As an author and editor myself, I am occasionally asked to review manuscripts for various publishers. To my surprise, the manuscript I received from UNTP was the completed version of the partial manuscript that Ella Szabó had asked me to read so many years before. Included with it was a cover letter saying that Ella had passed away in 2009. Before she died, Ella's family had promised her that they would endeavor to have the book published. And so they eventually sent the manuscript to UNTP.

After reading the entire manuscript, I recommended it for publication, with some revisions in the way the recipes were written and a few questions answered about place names, dates, and historical references. Several months later, Ella's husband, Arto Szabó, and their daughter, Eve Aino Roza Wirth, both contacted me by email to say they would make those revisions themselves and to ask if I would read the revised manuscript before it was returned to the publisher. But again, fate delayed that process. Family illnesses, relocations to other places, and the passing of Arto Szabó all put the cookbook project on hold once more.

Finally, Ella's daughter, Eve, was ready to move forward with her mother's legacy cookbook. And it's through my contact with Eve that I discovered what a remarkable person Ella Szabó had been and what an interesting life she had led.

The wedding of Ella Kovács
and Arto Olavi Szabó, 1962.

Ella Szabó with one of her special
cream cakes, 1960s.

Ella and her daughter, Eve, with
Ella's Walnut Wedding Torte baked
for the fiftieth anniversary of friends
in Greenwich, Connecticut, 1995.

Ella with her special Walnut
Wedding Torte, baked for the
wedding of friends in Dover,
Vermont, 2000.

Ella Kovács Szabó was born in Hungary in 1929 in a small town with a big name, Hódmezővásárhely, in the southern part of the country. Her father owned a store that sold agricultural supplies to local farmers, and her mother ran a kindergarten. The family owned a small orchard on the edge of town, and her father was known as a horticulturist who developed methods to improve the productivity of the region's fruit and nut orchards. Ella grew up to become an avid gardener herself, a lively woman who also loved sports, especially tennis, as well as classical music and ballet.

In 1952 Ella received a master's degree in physical education from the University of Physical Education in Budapest. Following in her mother's footsteps as a teacher, she became head of the physical education departments at two high schools in Hungary and a member of the Hungarian national women's basketball team. But when the Soviet military began crushing the Hungarian Revolution in 1956, she fled her home country, sneaking across the border at night into Austria and eventually crossing the Atlantic Ocean to New York on a US troop carrier.

After settling in New York City, Ella soon obtained positions as assistant physical education director for the Staten Island YMCA and the Yonkers YWCA, and then as head of the physical education department at the all-girl Lenox School in New York. In 1960 she was invited to join the US Olympic Synchronized Swimming Exhibition Team, which represented America in the Summer Olympics in Rome that year. And later she became a professor of physical education at City College of New York.

Ella met her husband-to-be, Arto Szabó—another refugee from the 1956 Hungarian Revolution—on the steps of the Free Magyar (Hungarian) Reformed Church in New York City. In 1962, six months after Ella had become an American citizen, they were married in that same church. And in the mid-1960s the couple moved to Greenwich, Connecticut, where they lived for the next four decades.

Ella was a small woman (only five feet, two inches tall) with a big heart. She developed menus and supervised food services for a homeless shelter. She baked countless cakes and tortes for weddings, church socials, and charity events. She gave baking classes and demonstrations at a variety of venues, appeared as a baking expert on radio shows, wrote food articles for the *Greenwich Time* and *Stamford Advocate* newspapers, and consulted with Rick Rodgers on the Hungarian tortes that appear in his cookbook

Kaffeehaus: Exquisite Desserts from Classic Cafés of Vienna, Budapest, and Prague (which includes one of her walnut torte recipes). In addition to being an active member of the International Association of Culinary Professionals, she was a fund raiser for Les Dames d'Escoffier (an international philanthropic organization of women leaders in the culinary field), served on the board of directors of the Connecticut Women's Culinary Alliance, and in 2002 was initiated into the National League of American Pen Women. She somehow also found time to be a slimnastics and tennis instructor for Norwalk Community College in Connecticut.

Ella Szabó was obviously a special person, with a loving husband, a doting daughter, and many friends. Baking was her passion, and, according to her daughter, Ella baked something almost every day. Who would have thought that a slim, athletic, Hungarian-born member of a US Olympic swimming team would also turn out to be an accomplished baker of Central European tortes? Maybe that's the secret recipe for eating your cake and staying svelte, too!

In 2002 Ella and her daughter Eve attended the three-day celebration of Julia Child's 90th birthday at Copia: The American Center for Wine, Food & the Arts, in Napa, California. Many years later, upon learning about my own minor connection with Julia Child, Eve wrote to me about that party for Julia. "We were fortunate to meet her that evening, and Mom told her all about this book. I'll never forget Julia telling my mom to 'never give up on your dreams!' So the story comes full circle now, to the miraculous way that Julia's memory and you have come back into our lives, helping to bring Mom's dream to fruition." And, thanks to the publishing staff at University of North Texas Press, the rest of us are now able to taste Ella Szabó's delicious dream too.

Sharon Hudgins
Editor

AUTHOR'S PREFACE

During the opulent era of the Austro-Hungarian Empire (1867–1918), when many recipes in this cookbook were created, Budapest was one of Europe's coffeehouse capitals (the other was Vienna), where tables were laden with extraordinary baked goods. A multitude of coffeehouses and pastry shops in Budapest served their clientele original cakes, pastries, and tortes, each a specialty of that particular place. At the turn of the twentieth century, professional pastry chefs and home bakers in Hungary were equally creative, and competition was often fierce among them to see who could come up with the newest and most unusual torte or pastry for a particular occasion. But sadly, many of their recipes were lost because of wars, economic hardships, and dislocations. The recipes in this book were almost lost, too, except for their fortuitous rescue shortly after World War II and, much later, a serendipitous meeting I had with the owner of this treasured culinary collection. After many years of our friendship, she entrusted me with her original heirloom recipes with the plea "to publish these recipes someday so they may be enjoyed by many."

Through this book I hope to be a conduit of culinary history, presenting personal, treasured Hungarian recipes—many of them never before published—to modern pastry chefs and home bakers. Over the years I have painstakingly translated, tested, streamlined, and retested these recipes to better suit today's busy American lifestyle. But the spirit and taste of these recipes remain true to their original source. In addition, I've created and added recipes for my own special-occasion tortes and pastries. I also introduce many of the recipes with some of their historical background or my own personal memories.

Many of these recipes are distinguished by their use of nut flour (finely ground nuts), which enhances the flavor of the other ingredients and imparts a luxurious texture and taste to these desserts. For people not allergic to nuts, nut flour contributes valuable nutrients and important minerals and makes the desserts edible for those who suffer from wheat allergies or gluten intolerance. The beautiful appearance of these desserts also evokes the elegance and gracious hospitality of the Old World, a Europe that now exists only in the fading memories of a few.

Elegant Hungarian Tortes and Homestyle Desserts for American Bakers presents the recipes for more than fifty authentic, original Hungarian cookies, cakes, pastries, and tortes, many of which would not have survived except for my dear Hungarian friend, Isabella Eckmayer, affectionately known as Belli Tante. The story of how these recipes weathered the winds of World War II and later came into my possession is remarkable in itself.

Ella Kovács Szabó
Greenwich, CT
2009

Editor's Note
The narrative was written, and the recipes in this cookbook tested, by Ella Kovács Szabó before her untimely passing in 2009. Her warm and personal reminiscences in the recipe headnotes add a valuable cultural and historical context to the recipes themselves. Additional material about ingredients, kitchen equipment, Hungarian specialties, and the family's history was contributed by her daughter, Eve Aino Roza Wirth, and by me with the approval of Ella Szabó's family.

INTRODUCTION

Mention Hungarian baking and most people think first of strudel or the spectacular multilayer Dobos Torte. However, there is another category of Hungarian specialties that until recently has been relatively unknown in the United States: tortes, pastries, cakes, and cookies made from nut flours instead of wheat flours. Torte, in particular, is the European term for a rich cake, often multilayered, that is usually made from nut flour (with or without bread crumbs or a little wheat flour, too) and often leavened (or raised) with stiffly beaten egg whites. Many tortes are filled with buttercreams or fruit jams and are fancily decorated with whipped cream, chocolate, jam, and candied fruits.

This book takes the modern baker on a journey to the kitchens of Hungary's past and present, opening up new horizons in the field of baking. Many of the recipes come from a cherished family collection that originated in the Austro-Hungarian kitchens of the Belle Époque, the period around the turn of the twentieth century from the 1890s to the start of World War I in 1914. They evoke an era of lavish parties and balls, opulent hotels, and elegant pastry shops. Budapest at the time was known as the Little Paris of the East, a capital city where fancy tortes and pastries were served for every occasion at every level of society. Even before that era, fabulous desserts were specially created for the occasion when Franz Liszt, the famous Hungarian composer and pianist, performed in Budapest, and when Count Esterházy's family invited friends to a concert by Franz Joseph Haydn, their court composer, at their magnificent Rococo palace in Fertőd, Hungary, fashioned after Louis XIV's château at Versailles.

Unfortunately, many of these recipes were lost in the wars and economic upheavals of the twentieth century, and the culinary arts continued to languish under Hungary's Communist system after World War II. Only after the change of government in 1989 have they revived again in Hungary, much to my delight. Coffeehouses and pastry shops once more abound not only in Budapest but also throughout the country, and several classic old coffeehouse-cafés—such as Auguszt, Gerbeaud, Ruszwurm, and Művész Kávéház in Budapest—are busier than ever.

COFFEEHOUSES AND PASTRY SHOPS

Coffee came to Hungary in the sixteenth century with the Ottoman Turks, whose conquest and occupation of Hungarian lands lasted for 150 years. During the seventeenth century, coffee—hot, black, and strong—became firmly entrenched as a favored stimulant in Hungary and eventually was even considered to be the country's national drink.

The seventeenth century saw the establishment of the first coffeehouses in Europe, places where men could gather to consume cups of the fashionable nonalcoholic brew. But the real heyday of coffeehouse culture, especially in Hungary and other parts of the Habsburg Empire, was from the second half of the nineteenth century until the beginning of World War I. To some extent the lure of the old coffeehouses remained, through social and economic upheavals, until the start of World War II. But in the postwar era of Communist Hungary, many of the traditional coffeehouses of Budapest and other Hungarian cities either closed or became mere shadows of their former selves.

In the late 1800s, however, coffeehouses were attractive and popular gathering places for members of the growing middle class, as well as penurious artists and writers, who could linger for hours over a cup of coffee in surroundings more spacious and lavishly furnished than their own humble homes: dark wood paneling, stylish bentwood chairs, cozy upholstered banquettes, cast-iron tables with marble tops, high ceilings and marble columns (faux and real), and large windows that let in a lot of light. The coffeehouse became an important social institution, frequented by painters and poets, theater performers and political activists, and a range of other literary, artistic, and political figures who spent much of their time in coffeehouses reading newspapers, writing essays, discussing important issues of the day, and even planning revolutions. In many ways, Europe's coffeehouses were the Starbucks of their era.

The menus at those old coffeehouses were fairly limited, although the variety of coffee choices was large— twenty or more different styles of coffee, from single to double espressos; coffee with varying amounts of milk or whipped cream; coffee spiked with brandy, rum, sweet liqueurs, vanilla ice cream, or an egg yolk (for hangovers); and real Turkish coffee, each cup individually boiled until foaming in a small, specially shaped copper pot, then brought to the table in its pot before being tipped into a tiny cup. Usually only simple cold meals were available in those coffeehouses, plus a limited selection of cakes and pastries.

Coffeehouses were almost entirely a male preserve. Until the late 1800s, women seldom ate or drank in public—and even then, only in the company of a man. Instead, they entertained women friends at home, often at afternoon gatherings where coffee or tea was served with cakes and pastries, either homemade or bought from a professional bakery. But in the 1890s government regulations in the Habsburg lands finally allowed bakeries of sweets to sell coffee on their premises—and it also became socially acceptable for women to eat in those public pastry-shop cafés, even without a man by their side.

Many of those cafés were modest little neighborhood businesses, with only a few tables and a small selection of sweets. Others, especially in the major cities, were luxuriously decorated temples of the bakers' art, with warm colors, ornate plasterwork, plenty of gilding, twinkling chandeliers, and long glass cases displaying an impressive variety of fancy cakes, tortes, and pastries. Women could meet their friends at those cafés for afternoon coffee, cake, and conversation without incurring the censure of society's watchdogs.[1]

Today, the nineteenth-century distinctions between coffeehouses and pastry shops have blurred considerably, with both kinds of public eateries offering similar drinks and desserts to a mixed clientele of men and women. Many coffeehouses have now morphed into restaurants serving a range of hot and cold meals. And some of the pastry-shop cafés even offer light meals, too. Fortunately, some of the traditional coffeehouses and elegant old pastry shops in Budapest—Gerbeaud, Ruszwurm, Auguszt, Café Central, Café New York—managed to survive wars, revolutions, and economic fluctuations and have now been restored to their former glory, where modern customers can bask in the nostalgia of times long past while enjoying a good cup of coffee and a luscious torte.

Editor

This cookbook presents more than fifty recipes for delicious, elegant treats served at Hungarian coffeehouses and pastry shops, as well as desserts made in the home kitchens of local cooks. Many of these recipes are made with nut flours—almond, walnut, and hazelnut—which give the tortes a unique texture and a rich, complex flavor. Nut flour is an ingredient often used instead of wheat flour to make the sponge-cake batter that is the base of many tortes. Nut flours can also be blended into the torte's filling, alone or with chocolate, fruit, or other ingredients. The names of these delicacies evoke memories not only of the flavors and textures of the past but also of the bakers who made these treats or the special people for whom they were created: Belli Tante's Apple Torte, Sári Fedák's Chestnut-Almond Torte, Isabella Torte, Esterházy Torte, and many more.

Over the years I have translated, tested, and retested the heirloom recipes in this book, in addition to developing many of my own. Despite the age and tradition of most of these recipes, I have been able to adapt them to accommodate today's busy lifestyles, streamlining the traditional methods for today's home bakers without compromising the authentic taste, texture, and appearance of these classic Hungarian desserts. The use of modern kitchen equipment has eased some of the previously laborious steps, and I have adapted some of the ingredients to better suit today's appliances. Many of these desserts can also be baked in advance and frozen for several months, with no change in taste or texture. Whether you're a novice or an expert, you will find desserts that you'll want to bake again and again.

The nutritional value of these delicacies from the past also provides an incentive to try them. Research tells us of the health benefits of the nuts traditionally used in Hungarian desserts, nuts that are rich in monounsaturated fats and also good sources of important minerals such as magnesium and potassium, as well as vitamin E. For people on gluten-free diets, the wheat-free desserts are just what the doctor ordered. These are also ideal to serve as Jewish Passover desserts.

This is the first time this collection of heirloom recipes has been published, and the story of how they came into my possession is quite remarkable.

Family Recipes Lost and Found

It was 1944 in Cservenka, Hungary, on a golden October afternoon. War was raging across Europe, but life continued, tranquil and carefree, in this multiethnic town on the fertile plains of the Vojvodina region. Judith Eckmayer was 15 years old, out playing tennis with her girl-friends. The group giggled and chatted about parties, boys, and the latest fashions. At home in the family garden, her mother, Isabella, was cutting roses for a vase as she prepared to host a circle of society ladies for tea. She had just baked a new Apple Torte and was looking forward to her guests' verdict; if they approved, Isabella would add it to her repertoire of recipes—a treasured, handwritten collection begun by her mother and bound in burgundy leather.

❋❋❋❋❋❋❋❋❋❋❋❋❋❋❋❋❋❋❋❋❋❋❋❋❋❋❋❋

CSERVENKA

Cservenka was a small town in the Vojvodina region of northeastern Serbia, populated by a mix of Serbs, Hungarians, and Germans. Since the seventeenth century, it had belonged to the territories of Austria-Hungary, and by 1910 the majority of the population was German-speaking. In the period between World Wars I and II, it belonged to the Kingdom of Yugoslavia, but during World War II, the region was annexed to Hungary under the Axis administration and occupied by Axis troops. In 1944 it was liberated by Soviet and Yugoslav forces, and at the end of the war, the ethnic German population was expelled from the town. After 1945 Cservenka became part of the People's Republic of Serbia within Communist Yugoslavia. Today it belongs to the independent country of Serbia, where its name is Crvenka (population 9,000).[2]

Editor

❋❋❋❋❋❋❋❋❋❋❋❋❋❋❋❋❋❋❋❋❋❋❋❋❋❋❋❋

But Isabella would not be welcoming friends into her garden for tea and torte that day—or ever again. Two German soldiers were at the gate. They belonged to a Wehrmacht unit withdrawing from the Balkans in the face of the Soviet army's advance. And they were there to warn her: Russian troops would overrun Cservenka in a matter of days. Isabella's family had much to fear. Her husband, the director of one of Central Europe's largest sugar factories, was Austrian. After Germany's annexation of Austria in 1938, the family had become nationals of the German Reich. To Russian troops, they were enemy citizens.

The German soldiers offered to help the family evacuate. Their unit was retreating to Vienna, 460 kilometers (285 miles) away. Isabella's husband was away on business, so the family's fate was in her hands. She packed valuables into a small suitcase and sewed her jewels into her daughter's winter coat. At dawn the next morning, Judith left Cservenka inside a Wehrmacht ambulance. Isabella stayed behind with her elderly mother, who was too frail to endure the arduous journey.

As predicted, Cservenka was soon under Soviet military rule. In her husband's absence, Isabella was arrested and jailed for six months until the war ended in Hungary in April 1945. Upon her release Isabella learned that her mother had died of pneumonia. Her husband had managed to flee to Vienna and was with Judith there.

When she returned to the family home, Isabella found it entirely empty, ransacked by Russian soldiers. All that remained were picture hooks on the bare walls. As she went from room to room in despair, she spied through her tears an unfinished petit-point pillow that she had been embroidering with a Raphael Madonna, lying on the floor. Under it lay her beloved recipe collection. As she picked it up, she felt a tinge of triumph. "You may have taken away my worldly possessions," she exclaimed, "but you have left what I value most—my recipe collection!"

Fast forward from 1945 to 1969, thirteen years after I had moved to America from Hungary, and seven years after I married my husband, Arto Szabó, also a Hungarian who had emigrated to the United States in 1956. One day we decided to go to Island Beach, a little island off the shore of Greenwich, the town where we now lived in Connecticut—and good fortune, or fate, came into play.

We were ready for a day of fun at the beach. My husband's brother, Miklós, and his wife, Evá, had just arrived from Hungary, and we were eager to show them all the charms of our hometown in our adopted country. Eve, our daughter, was just three years old at the time, and I well remember putting a little pink hat on her blond hair to protect her from the sun. Off she went with her pail of toys to play in the sand. Shortly after she chose her spot and settled in, a little brunette girl sat down next to her. Before we knew it, they were playing together as if they had known each other their whole lives.

At lunchtime we called Eve to join us at our picnic table. The two little girls had to part, but as it turned out, not for long. Eve ran to us and the other little girl went to her family, whose table on the beach happened to be right next to ours. Incredibly, it sounded as though they were speaking Hungarian. How wonderful, I thought, another Hungarian family! And the two little girls had already met. It didn't take long before we grown-ups introduced ourselves too.

That is how I met Judith Eckmayer-Wedow, the woman who was to become my dearest friend, and her dashing husband, Janusz, their daughter,

Julie, and most important for this book, Judith's mother, Isabella. Family and friends called her Belli Tante, *Belli* being short for Isabella, and *Tante* being the German word for aunt.

Belli Tante was born in 1896 in Osijek, Kingdom of Croatia-Slavonia (within the Austro-Hungarian Empire at that time). When she was growing up, her parents were the owners of the Nádor, a fashionable grand hotel in the Hungarian city of Pécs. It was as manager of the hotel that Belli Tante's mother began collating recipes of tortes popular across the Austro-Hungarian Empire. Her hotel was famous, her standards high. Growing up, Belli Tante was practically weaned on the most sumptuous pastries imaginable. She traveled frequently to Budapest, vacationed at Lake Balaton, and met her future husband, an officer of the Habsburg Army, in a bustling garrison town. After the end of World War II in 1945, she left Hungary to join her family in Austria, moving between cities before settling in the capital, Vienna. Everywhere she went, she collected torte recipes: the favorites of friends and acquaintances, of old aristocratic families, and of young cooks employed in her kitchens. Some of the recipes were tried and tested, others invented for a special occasion. Each and every one represented memories of the celebrations and daily lives of the people who prepared and enjoyed them.

Belli Tante's handwritten recipe (in German) for
Hungary's famous Dobos Torte.

Isabella Schaffer (with two
unidentified girls), Hungary, 1914.

Isabella Schaffer, Hungary, 1914.

Ella Szabó with Judith Eckmayer-
Wedow, Isabella (Belli Tante)
Eckmayer's daughter, Provence,
France, 1998.

Isabella Schaffer Eckmayer
with her husband, Fritz Eckmayer,
Bela Crkva, Hungary, 1917.

In 1968 Belli Tante moved to America to live with her daughter's family, the Wedows, in Connecticut. Many were the times that we visited the Wedow household, and many were the times that Belli Tante greeted us with a freshly baked torte accompanied by a special tea imported from Vienna. Growing up in Hungary, I had often eaten traditional tortes, but Belli Tante's were unique; I had never tasted anything like them before.

Take, for instance, her Apple Torte. The base was made with almond flour ground by hand, and the result was a dessert that balanced and blended the flavors and textures of almonds, apples, vanilla, and apricots to a divine perfection. To be honest, "heavenly" is only a slice of what I could say about how this wonderful torte tasted.

After I got to know her, Belli Tante told me the secret of these tortes: flour made not from grains but from nuts that were finely ground by hand—almonds, hazelnuts, and walnuts, some of them blanched and toasted before grinding. Years later, she gave me all her treasured recipes, rescued after World War II—a priceless collection of Hungarian tortes and pastries from the turn of the twentieth century. "I want you to publish these recipes someday, because I want them to be enjoyed by many people," she told me. "You are the one who can do it."

And so I began to test the recipes and adapt them to modern American kitchens. I was thrilled when my friend Sally Gundy, whom I'd known for many years, agreed to help with the translations and testing. We had originally met in New York, when I was head of the physical education department at a small, private girls' school and Sally was my assistant. We became such good friends that Sally was maid of honor at my wedding. Later Sally and I lost track of each other for a few years, and when we met again she was teaching German. What luck! Most of Belli Tante's recipes were written not in Hungarian but in German, which was the main language of the multilingual Austro-Hungarian Empire.

Sally and I became a team: she translated the recipes that were written in German, and together we tested all of them, meeting once a week for four years. Translating the measurements was an especially tedious job, because each of the European-style metric weights had to be recalculated in American cups and spoons. Countess Éva Edelsheim Gyulai of Hungary also helped with the translations, through letters sent back and forth by mail.

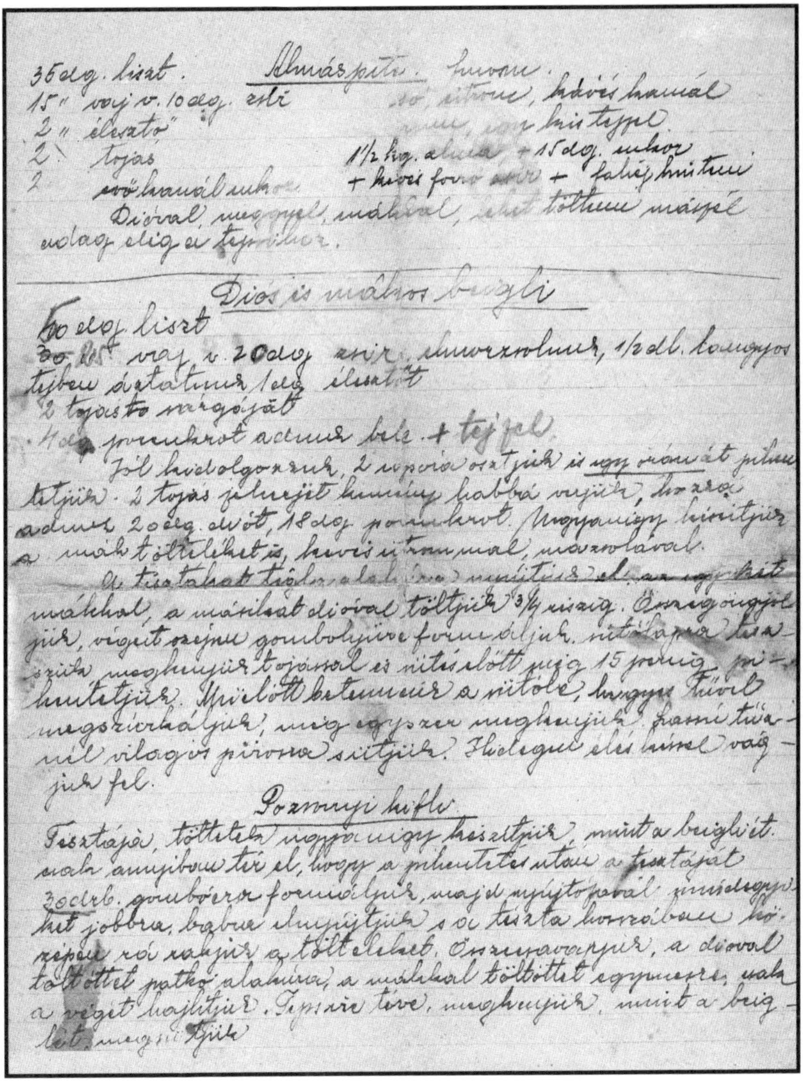

36 dkg. liszt.   Almáspite.
15" vaj v. 10 dkg. zsír
2 " élesztő"
2 " tojás
2   sörhamával [illegible]

Diós és mákos bejgli

50 dkg liszt
30 dkg vaj v. 20 dkg zsír [illegible]
2 tojás [illegible]

[several lines of illegible handwritten Hungarian text]

Pozsonyi kifli

[several lines of illegible handwritten Hungarian text]

Handwritten recipes (in Hungarian) by Ella's mother, Roza Kovács.

CAKE OR TORTE?

Tortes are a type of **cake** but are distinctively different enough to rate a baking category all their
own. Although the boundaries between **cakes**
and **tortes** are sometimes blurred, there are several
general principles governing which is which (most
of the time).

Cakes are traditionally made with butter (or oil),
whole eggs, sugar, and wheat flour, with additional
flavorings such as vanilla, chocolate, lemon, or many
others. The leavening agent that causes them to rise
in the oven can be baking powder, baking soda, or
sometimes beaten egg whites. Cakes are baked in
many different sizes and shapes, usually with two to
four relatively thick layers that are then sandwiched
together with icing or frosting, covered with frosting
on the outside too, and decorated in a great variety
of ways. Cakes are generally lighter in texture and
taller in height than tortes, but there are exceptions to
this (and every other) rule.

Most **tortes** are made with finely ground nuts (nut meal
or nut flour) instead of wheat flour, although the torte
batters sometimes also include dry bread crumbs,
cracker crumbs, cake crumbs, or even a small amount
of wheat flour. The batter is usually leavened only by
well-beaten whole eggs or stiffly beaten egg whites.
Tortes are often denser and moister in texture than
other kinds of cakes—and richer in flavor—although
some tortes can be lighter textured. And since the
ingredients for most tortes can be expensive (especially all those nuts), tortes are often considered more
elegant than standard cakes.

Tortes are usually round in shape, but some are
square or rectangular. Many simple tortes consist of

only one layer, which is often brushed with a sweet glaze, coated with a thin, smooth layer of icing, or simply dusted with confectioners' sugar. Others are multilayered and more complex, such as the famous Hungarian Dobos Torte, with its five thin layers of vanilla sponge cake alternating with thin layers of chocolate buttercream and topped with a caramel glaze, and Hungarian Esterházy Torte, with many thin layers of nutty baked-meringue (*dacquoise*) alternating with layers of boozy buttercream filling, all topped with white fondant decorated with a chocolate spiderweb pattern. Other tortes, whether single- or multilayered, are crowned with berries, toasted nuts, whipped cream, or meringue.

Hence, even though all **tortes** are **cakes**—not all **cakes** are **tortes**.

Editor

SPONGE CAKES

Cakes can be divided into two basic types: dense and moist in texture, or light, airy, and foamy, depending on the ingredients and techniques used in making them. Several kinds of cakes belong to the latter category, an ensemble known as **sponge cakes**, each with different characteristics and uses—but all of them known as sponge cakes because of their light, airy texture.

Sponge cakes were originally made with only flour, sugar, and eggs, with the eggs, whole or separated into yolks and whites, beaten for a long time to incorporate air into them, which makes the cake rise in the oven. Eventually cooks began adding other ingredients to the basic sponge mixture, such as butter, vegetable oil, baking powder, cornstarch, cream of tartar, and any number of flavorings, resulting in the variety of cakes called sponges today.

Sponge cake batters made with nut flours replacing all (or most) of the wheat flour in standard sponge cake recipes form the basis of many European tortes. Many of the torte recipes in this book use one or the other of these two basic techniques for making classic sponge cakes:

- **Biscuit** (French term, pronounced *bees-QWEE*): A type of sponge cake in which the egg yolks and whites are separated, with the egg yolks beaten until pale yellow and thick, then the sugar gradually beaten into the yolks before the flour (or nut flour) is folded into the mixture. Lastly, the stiffly beaten egg whites are folded into the batter, making a cake that is especially light and airy (and nothing like American or British biscuits, despite the same name).

- **Genoise** (French term, pronounced *zhen-WAHZ*): A sponge cake made with whole eggs (not separated) combined with sugar and warmed in the top of a double boiler while being beaten until pale yellow, fluffy, and doubled or tripled in volume, before the flour (or nut flour) is folded into them. Classic *genoises* usually have melted butter folded into the batter just before baking, too, but many nut-flour *genoises* do not because the nuts contain so much fat (nut oil) themselves.

Both of these kinds of **sponge cake** are also suitable for making flat cakes baked on a sheet pan, then rolled up around a custard, buttercream, or jam filling, as in the several Hungarian roulade recipes in this book.

Editor

I also learned to make nut flours in my own kitchen. In Hungary every household had a simple hand-operated nut grinder; I can remember my mother and grandmother using theirs. But I realized that in order to truly fulfill Belli Tante's wish to make the recipes enjoyable to all, I would also have to also adapt the recipes to suit the modern American baker. As I experimented, I developed a method of preparing a nut-flour sponge-cake base (called for in many of the recipes) without separating the eggs (as required in many sponge-cake recipes). So some of the recipes are easier to make than in Belli Tante's time, but they preserve the taste and texture of those labor-intensive Old World desserts.

In addition to adapting Belli Tante's collection of recipes, I collected other heirloom recipes from family, friends, and a few famous Hungarian pastry shops whose quality matched those of Belli Tante's. The result is this book, a composite collection of time-tested traditional Hungarian desserts, including such classics as Esterházy Torte, Walnut or Poppy-Seed *Beigli*, and Gerbeaud Slices.

At one time it was also the fashion for tortes to be created for special occasions. My friend Judith Eckmayer-Wedow told me that after she recovered from a childhood illness, the doctor's wife, Mrs. Müller, created a special torte in her honor. Even as I was testing Belli Tante's recipes, I began to follow the example of Budapest society and create tortes of my own to celebrate special occasions. For the rehearsal dinner for our daughter Eve's wedding, I created the Coffee-Almond Torte as the groom's torte for her soon-to-be husband, Russell. When my grandsons Russell and Spencer were born, I baked this delicious torte again for their christenings. And whenever I prepared for a trip to visit my family in California, I asked my two little grandsons what they would like me to bring. "Books? Toys?" I asked. "Tortes and cookies, please, Nana!" was always their reply.

Each time, when testing my own recipes or Belli Tante's or those from famous Budapest pastry shops, I called on our family and friends to taste the results. "Do you like it?" I would ask, hoping the answer was yes. The response was always encouraging: "More, please." Thank heavens my dear husband, Arto, loved sweets too.

And so I am delighted to present these treasured recipes for Hungarian tortes and other desserts that were handed down through generations, survived wars, were carried across an ocean, and finally were passed on to me. Now I offer them to the home bakers and pastry chefs of today—and tomorrow. Some of these tortes are for the novice baker; others are for the expert. All are delicious, and all are for those cooks who value keeping traditions alive. Many families have enjoyed them in Hungary in the past, long before our families enjoyed them in America. I'm sure that you, your families, and your friends will now also delight in eating these special Hungarian treats.

OF HUNGER AND ORANGES

She wanders along the highway, hopefully toward Vienna. She has escaped from the camp in Austria where her fellow Hungarian refugees sat, waiting for whatever happens next. She loathed the barbed-wire fences and the feeling that no matter what she did, she could not get out. Having finally reached a free land, she never dreamed she would find herself back in the same situation: an armed guard standing at the gate of the camp, and without proper documents, no one permitted to leave. "There are already too many Hungarians in Vienna," they were told. "We can't allow more refugees to drift in from the rural camps."

But she wants to get out of Europe as soon as possible— to leave the place where some killer instinct always possesses its peoples, or some government's hunger for power drags smaller nations into deadly war. No, she has had enough of this: first a world war, then Communism, and now a revolution.

So she walks along the highway, carrying a small satchel containing nothing more than a few pairs of underwear, a couple of photos, and some miscellaneous mementos. She is determined to reach Vienna and personally arrange her own passage out of Europe through the American Embassy.

The wintry dusk slowly begins to settle in, and lights start to flicker on warmly, invitingly, in the village houses along the road. A gentle breeze carries with it delicious aromas of dinnertime. She draws in a deep breath of fresh air to muster extra strength, and she starts to think that perhaps life will be worth living after all. And she wonders what she still needs to do, what is still waiting for her ahead.

18

A clanking noise awakens her from her daydreaming. A truck approaches. How good it would be, she thinks, if she could catch a ride for a few kilometers.

The truck slows to a stop next to her, before she even starts to flag it down, and a friendly Austrian man calls out to her something like, "Where are you headed, young lady?" Her heart leaps. Could it be that compassion and understanding still exist in the human heart?

After lengthy attempts to explain herself, hindered by her scant knowledge of the German language, she finally manages to get across that she is trying to go to Vienna. She jumps in the truck and an hour later is dropped off on the outskirts of Vienna, not a penny in her pocket and knowing scarcely more than a few words in German.

She doesn't know a soul there and knows nothing of the city, either. But she cannot just stand there on the corner alone, waiting for the morning, so she jumps on the first tram that approaches, headed toward the center of Vienna.

With the tinkling of the tram and the friendly face of the conductor, for a moment she forgets how alone she is. Slowly, ever so gently, a light snow begins to fall, as if to welcome her, a homeless child of an orphaned little nation, on this December night. With a renewed sense of wonder and curiosity, she watches the lights and expensive window displays as the trolley hurries ahead. On this corner, Christmas trees for sale—even silver ones! On that corner, an enormous store filled with toys and a café packed with customers. And up ahead, an entire street lit up, and over there a theater, and over there a museum! She jerks her head back and forth, back and forth, desperate to see every-thing, relishing every sight and sound, still unable to believe her eyes, that all this exists, that all this is true. How different from the Hungary she had left!

A couple stand up and begin pushing through the crowded tram, struggling toward the exit, laden with packages. Amid the bustle an orange drops to the floor, unnoticed. An orange! In her own country, she hadn't seen an orange in ten years, let alone any kind of tropical fruit. Oh, how wondrous, how amazing it would be to lean down, pick it up, and eat it. Then suddenly she realizes how desperately hungry she is. If only there weren't so many people on the tram. She is ashamed of herself. The tram conductor had already let her ride for free; what more did she want? She had made it to a free land, she'd even managed to leave the refugee camp—and now she wants the orange, too?

The next curve in the tracks settles the question for her: the orange rolls out the door and off the tram. She wants to leap after it, but it's too late.

It is snowing harder now and already dark outside, because night comes early in the winter. She is enjoying the snowfall. She'd always loved the snow, and she recalls the time when her father pulled her and her siblings in their brand-new sled to the winter market to eat roasted chestnuts. He had lined the sled with blankets and hot stones to keep the children from catching cold. It was snowing then, too.

Chestnuts were one thing, but now where is even a morsel of bread that she can eat? And where will she sleep this night?

The hunger pangs are becoming unbearable. She starts to slump, tears welling in her eyes, feeling again how utterly alone she is.

The tram pulls up to the next stop. Maybe she should get off. She can't ride it to the end of the world, after all.

20

Besides, what difference does it make anyway? She will have to spend the night walking the streets no matter where she gets off. She notices a beautiful winter coat in a window display, sizing it up. Yes, it looks very warm and so attractive. But when would she ever be able to have such a lovely coat, or even just a coat that blocks out the wind?

Her gaze now falls on a young couple. She notices them stopping in front of a jewelry store and standing there, talking, then going inside and trying on rings. How wonderful it must be for them, she thinks. They're happy, safe, carefree. And here she stands, utterly alone, nothing to lean on, yet holding tight to her powerful faith that in the New World she will find happiness.

As she walks she finds herself slowing down in front of the food stores. She walks back and forth past them several times, finally stopping at one, and then—she isn't even sure how it happens—suddenly finding herself inside. What does she even want? She has no money and . . . wait . . . can it be? She looks up to see a friendly faced old woman smiling back at her, and she is overcome with emotion, reminded of her beloved mother still at home back in Hungary. She hesitates for a moment, then slowly heads to the exit.

A clerk stops her suddenly at the door. "Pardon? No, I didn't buy anything." The clerk is trying to hand her a bag full of food. She doesn't understand. "What? You're saying this bag is mine? But . . ." And then it slowly dawns on her: the kindly old lady, the one with the friendly face, the one who had smiled at her . . . she bought these groceries for her.

She tries to say something, something in the way of a thank you, and then, without even waiting for an answer, she runs out of the store. She sprints to the nearest bench, sweeps off the snow, and, sobbing, tears open the bag of food and lets out a gasp.

Among the items in the bag is a beautiful orange like the one she coveted earlier on the tram.

She doesn't even know where to start, what to eat first, how much, how quickly, whether to sate the hunger stabbing at her belly or indulge in the precious drops of juice from the orange in the bag.

Later, on this same night, finally outside the American Embassy, she takes her place in the long queue of refugees waiting to register for passage to the United States. It is bitterly cold, and the icy wind penetrates her thin winter coat, blowing through her. Finally, at 5:00 a.m., she makes it into the building and is assigned a place at one of the nearby refugee camps to wait for her departures to the United States. And at that moment she realizes that without the gift of that orange and ham and loaf of bread, she would not have had the strength to make it here.

Now, three years later, looking back on that journey as a refugee who finally found a haven in America, with a heart full of gratitude she gives thanks for all the good she has received, and wishes that God may bless those who, then and now, are able to recognize human suffering and step up to help.

Epilogue by Eve Aino Roza Wirth, Ella's Daughter

After a journey by sea from Europe, Ella saw Lady Liberty on the horizon, standing proud, welcoming her to her new home, the United States of America. When she disembarked the troop carrier that had brought her across the Atlantic Ocean, Ella was greeted at the dock by welcoming Americans and was handed a Coca-Cola—and an orange.

By Ella Szabó (writing under the pseudonym K. E. Bogatfalvi), published in June 1960. Translated from the Hungarian by Julie Tomasz and edited by Sharon Hudgins.

INGREDIENTS, EQUIPMENT, AND TECHNIQUES

by
Sharon Hudgins, Editor

Ingredients

Using the right ingredients, in the correct amounts, is essential for the success of recipes, especially those for baked goods like the tortes, cakes, cookies, and pastries in this book. The following basic ingredients were used in testing these recipes:

- **Eggs:** Grade A large eggs.

- **Wheat flour:** All-purpose white flour (bleached).

- **Nut flours:** See following section ("Nut Flours").

- **Milk:** Full-fat cows' milk (4% fat, whole milk).

- **Whipping cream:** Heavy whipping cream (36% to 40% fat).

- **Butter:** Good-quality unsalted butter. For your convenience, butter measurements in each recipe are given in four forms, based on: 1 standard stick of American butter = 4 ounces (weight), or 8 tablespoons, or ½ cup (volume).

- **Chocolate:** Some recipes use semi-sweet chocolate, grated and usually melted. Semi-sweet chocolate is sold in the form of bars by weight (ounces, pounds). Use the amount of chocolate, by weight, required in the recipe (not measured in cups or fractions of a cup).

- **Alcohol:** Several recipes use alcohol (such as brandy or liqueurs) as a flavoring, especially in icings and fillings. Alcohol enhances the nut or fruit flavor without making the pastry or torte boozy. You can certainly omit the alcohol, but if you have no aversion to it, try making the recipe with it to achieve the most authentic flavor.

Nuts and Nut Flours

Nuts are a major ingredient in many of the recipes in this book—especially almonds, hazelnuts (filberts), and walnuts—often finely ground into nut flour.

Nuts are sold still inside their shells or with the shells removed. Shelled nuts are packaged whole (with or without their papery skins attached), chopped, sliced, or ground into nut flour. Shelled nuts with their skins on are called natural or unblanched, whereas those without their skins are called blanched or skinned. (Almonds are usually referred to as blanched, whereas hazelnuts are skinned. Walnuts are not usually blanched or skinned, except for certain recipes, such as those for spiced or candied walnuts.)

Since nuts contain a large amount of fat, which can turn stale or rancid, it's best to buy whole nuts because they stay fresh longer. Store nuts (without their shells) in sealed, airtight plastic bags in your freezer to keep them fresh even longer. Always thaw frozen nuts or nut flours before using them in a recipe.

▶ **Toasted nuts:** Nuts, blanched or unblanched, are often toasted in the oven to enhance their flavor. Some of Ella Szabó's recipes indicate that the nuts used in them should be toasted, because toasting imparts the desired flavor; other recipes do not require toasting the nuts.

A general rule of thumb is to toast nuts in a single layer on a rimmed baking sheet in a preheated 350°F oven for about 10 minutes, shaking the pan occasionally until the nuts are lightly browned and you can smell their nutty aroma. Let them cool completely on the pan before using. Toasting time in the oven depends on the type of nut, its size, its fat content, and whether the nuts are whole, chopped, or sliced. Whole nuts need more time in the oven than nuts that have been cut.

▶ **Almonds:** Shelled almonds are available in several forms: whole (blanched or unblanched), chopped, slivered (the blanched whole nut cut lengthwise into matchstick-size pieces), and sliced or flaked (the whole nut sliced lengthwise into very thin, flat pieces).

- **To blanch whole almonds:** Pour boiling water over unblanched almonds in a heatproof bowl. Let them sit for about 5 minutes or until the brown skins begin to wrinkle on the nuts. Drain well, then submerge the nuts in cold water until they are cool enough to handle. Drain well again. Use your thumb and index finger to squeeze each almond, forcing the ivory-colored nut to slip out from the brown skin. Place the blanched almonds in a single layer on paper towels and let them dry overnight. The nuts must be completely dry before using them in a recipe.

  To speed up the drying process, spread the blanched almonds in a single layer on a rimmed baking sheet. Warm on the middle rack of a preheated 150°F oven for about 45 minutes, stirring them occasionally. Then bite into one almond, and if it still feels moist, dry them for another 10 minutes. Let the almonds cool completely on the pan before using them.

▶ **Hazelnuts:** Shelled hazelnuts are usually sold whole, blanched or unblanched (skinned or unskinned), because chopped hazelnuts become stale more quickly.

- **To blanch and toast hazelnuts:** Spread unblanched nuts in a single layer on a rimmed baking sheet set on the middle rack of a preheated 350°F oven. Toast the nuts for about 20 minutes, shaking the pan occasionally to ensure even toasting, until the papery brown skins have

Toasted hazelnuts are an ingredient in several torte recipes.

split and you can smell the nuts' toasty aroma.

Carefully pour the nuts onto a clean kitchen towel. Wrap the towel tightly around the nuts and place it in a clean plastic bag. Tie the bag shut and let the nuts cool for about 20 minutes. Then vigorously rub the nuts in the closed bag. Remove the nuts (still in the closed towel) from the plastic bag and continue to rub them in the towel to remove the skins. Don't worry if a few pieces of brown skins remain on the nuts. That won't affect the flavor. Let the nuts cool completely before using them. (They will already have been toasted during the blanching process.)

▶ **Walnuts:** In most cases, it's not necessary to toast walnuts before using them in a recipe, chopped or ground into nut flour, but toasting does enhance the flavor. Toast in a single layer on a rimmed baking sheet on the middle rack of a preheated 350°F oven for about 10 to 12 minutes, shaking the pan occasionally. Cool before using. If walnuts are to be used as decorations on cakes or tortes, it's always best to toast them first.

▶ **Nut flours:** Many of the recipes in this book require nut flour—nuts finely ground into a light-textured flour—which gives a unique taste and texture to the tortes and pastries. Many of the tortes are made entirely with nut flours instead of wheat flour, which also makes them gluten free. (For additional gluten-free suggestions, see the "Techniques" section.)

In the United States, commercial producers use two different terms for nuts that have been ground into finer pieces, which can cause confusion for home cooks. "Nut flour" often refers to ground blanched nuts (especially almonds), whereas "nut meal" refers to ground unblanched nuts, those with their papery brown skins still attached. For instance, almond flour is pale ivory in color, whereas almond meal is speckled brown from the skins included in the grind.

On the other hand, sometimes "nut flour" refers to very finely ground nuts (blanched or unblanched), while "nut meal" refers to a coarser grind of nuts. However, some commercial manufacturers use both terms on their packages. Hence the confusion between these two terms.

This book uses the term "nut flour" for the ground nuts required in the recipes, including almonds either blanched or unblanched. In addition, grinding the nuts by hand or with an electric kitchen appliance (such as a food processor),

Ella's grandson Spencer grinding nuts by hand in his mother's kitchen.

or grinding them in a large industrial machine in a factory, will affect the size of the grind and texture of the nut flour. Hand-ground nuts tend to be lighter and fluffier than those ground by a machine, which are somewhat heavier and denser. The type of grind will also affect the texture of the torte, cake, or pastry, with hand-ground nuts producing a lighter texture and machine-ground nuts making a slightly denser product.

Like all good Hungarian home cooks, Ella Szabó believed in grinding the nuts into flour by hand, using a nut grinder with a holder for the nuts and a rotary drum grater turned by hand or powered by electricity. Hungarian kitchens of the past were often equipped with a heavy metal, hand-operated grinder/grater that clamped onto the edge of a table or countertop. Today you can buy both inexpensive tabletop or countertop grinders that attach with a suction cup on the base and electric-powered grinder attachments for your stand mixer. (See recommendations for nut grinders in the "Equipment" section.)

Another option is to grind the nuts in a food processor. Grind only ½ cup of coarsely chopped nuts at a time, along with ½ teaspoon of sugar taken from the total amount of sugar required for the recipe. Pulse the nuts and sugar together in *very short bursts*—only 1 or 2 seconds at a time—so they don't become overprocessed and turn into oily nut butter (like peanut butter). After grinding each ½ cup of nuts, transfer them to a bowl and grind the remaining nuts as directed—always ½ cup of nuts at a time, together with ½ teaspoon of sugar.

You can also buy commercially ground nuts, which are much more available today than when Ella Szabó first started baking. National brands of nut flours such as King Arthur and Bob's Red Mill are sold in many stores, from upscale Whole Foods Market to your local Walmart. Less expensive house brands are also available at some stores, such as Costco. And many other brands can be ordered online.

▶ **Toasting nut flours:** Nut flours can also be toasted before using in a recipe, to make the nutty flavor even richer. Although some of Ella Szabó's recipes use toasted nut flour, most of them do not. However, if you prefer to toast the flour first, for the added flavor, it will work fine in any of her recipes.

Spread the nut flour in an even layer on a rimmed baking sheet and toast on the middle rack of a preheated 350°F oven for about 5 to 7 minutes, or until it just begins to brown and has the aroma of toasted nuts. Transfer the nut flour to a shallow bowl to cool completely before using.

▶ **Gluten-free:** All nut flours are naturally gluten free. However, if you must avoid wheat—especially if you have been diagnosed with celiac disease—and are concerned about cross-contamination of commercially made products, avoid purchasing nut flours that are processed and/or packaged in a facility that also processes other food allergens, including wheat. That information should be included on the package, so check carefully before you buy. (If the nut flour has been processed in a gluten-free facility, that information will be on the package.) To be safe, it is best to grind the nuts yourself, using one of the grinders recommended in the "Equipment" section.

▶ **IMPORTANT: Hand-ground nut flours versus commercially made nut flours:** For the recipes in this book, volume measurements (in cups) of *nut flours* are an approximation, to the nearest fraction of a cup, based on grinding the amount of *whole nuts* listed in the recipe.

Volume measurements of nut flours can vary slightly, depending on the size of the nuts and the method used for grinding them. Since hand-ground nut flours are fluffier and less dense than store-bought nut flours, the volume of hand-ground nut flour can be slightly larger than the volume of store-bought nut flour, even though they both weigh the same. Likewise, tortes made with commercially ground nut flours tend to be a bit denser than those made with nuts ground by hand.

For best results measure out the amount of *whole nuts* needed in a recipe (in cups, or by weight in ounces), then grind them in your own kitchen and use the amount of nut flour that you produce. If using *store-bought nut flour*, then use the number of cups of *nut flour* specified in the recipe.

Equipment

If you do a lot of baking, it's worthwhile to invest in the right equipment. Recipes in this book use the following pans, utensils, and appliances. Most of these items are not expensive and will last a lifetime.

- **Baking pans:** A variety of round and rectangular metal baking pans. Always use the correct pan size indicated in the recipe.

  Round springform pans (with removable sides), 8 inches, 9 inches, and 10 inches in diameter
  10 × 15–inch jelly-roll pan (with a small rim)
  11 × 17–inch rimmed baking sheet
  Flat cookie sheet (with no rim)

- **Baking parchment:** Oven-proof paper for lining baking pans and cookie sheets to prevent batters and doughs from sticking. If using parchment paper from a roll, which tends to curl up on your pan, lightly butter the pan first so the paper will stick to it.

- **Pastry cutter:** Semicircular utensil with a handle on the straight end and several curved narrow blades or wires attached to the handle. The pastry cutter is pushed back and forth through a flour-and-fat mixture to blend the dry ingredients with the butter (or other fat).

- **Offset metal spatulas:** Handy for smoothing the top of cake batter in the pan before baking, spreading the filling on cake layers, and frosting the top and sides of tortes and cakes.

- **Pastry bag:** Plastic-lined cloth bag with several interchangeable decorating tips for piping whipped cream or frosting onto cakes and tortes as decorations (stars, leaves, ruffles, flowers, etc.).

- **Other utensils:** Metal whisks, flexible rubber or silicone spatulas, wire cooling racks, free-standing oven thermometer.

- **Cake leveler/slicer:** Utensil for horizontally slicing cakes into even layers, preferably with one or more adjustable, serrated blades.

- **Cake comb:** Flat piece of metal or plastic, with one smooth edge and one or more serrated edges; the straight edge is used for smoothing the icing on a cake and the serrated edges for making decorative lines on icing.

- **Cake rounds (or cake boards):** Heavy cardboard rounds, usually coated on one side with plastic wrap or foil, as single-use, disposable serving platters for tortes and cakes.

- **Cake doilies:** Pretty round, square, or rectangular lace-paper doilies, usually white, placed on the serving platter before the cake or torte is set on it, as an added decorative touch.

- **Cake dome (or cake cover):** Large glass or plastic cover shaped to fit over a cake without touching it. Used for protecting cakes on counters and in the refrigerator. Some plastic cake covers have a clip-on base, turning the two-part assembly into a handy cake carrier. You can also use a very large mixing bowl as a cake cover.

- **Kitchen scale:** For weighing ingredients, especially the nuts used for grinding into nut flours. (Professional bakers weigh all of their dry ingredients—flour, sugar, nuts, spices—instead of measuring them with cups and spoons as most home bakers do. Measuring dry ingredients by weight is actually more accurate.)

- **Electric mixers:** Most recipes in this book use an electric stand mixer with a 5- or 6-quart bowl, which makes mixing the ingredients faster and easier. Some recipes use a stand mixer for one step and a handheld electric mixer for another step. If you don't have a stand mixer, you can use a handheld electric mixer for all steps of the recipes, although it might take slightly longer to beat the ingredients to the required consistency.

- **Electric food processor:** Especially as a tool for grinding nuts into nut flour.

- **Nut grinders:** For grinding whole nuts into nut flour. Several types—both hand operated and electric—are available at cookware stores and from online vendors. Purchase one that has a rotating metal drum (with holes in it) for grinding nuts (these are also describe as cheese graters), *not* one that has horizontal blades used for chopping nuts.

Some of the hand-operated grinders currently available online are the Geedel Rotary Cheese Grater with 3 Interchangeable Blades, the Vekaya Rotary Cheese Grater and Shredder, the Cambom Rotary Cheese Grater/Shredder/Chopper, the Keouke Manual Rotary Cheese Grater/Veggie Slicer/Shredder/Nut Grinder, and the Foodie Rotary Cheese Grater/Nut Grinder with Handle. All of these are priced at less than thirty dollars. They have a large suction cup on the bottom for attaching the grinder to a countertop and a handle on the side for rotating the grinder drum, and are very easy to use.

Mouli, Zyliss, and Vivaant all make handheld cheese graters/nut grinders with rotary drums. However, these are more labor-intensive, take longer to grind a large amount of nuts, and sometimes produce an uneven grind with several nut pieces much larger than the rest of the nuts ground into flour. You have to regrind those larger pieces to obtain a consistently textured nut flour.

Some of the electric-powered cheese graters/nut grinders available online include the Cofun Slicer/Shredder Attachment for KitchenAid Stand Mixers, the Homdox Electric Cheese Grater/Professional Salad Shooter/Electric Slicer/Shredder; and the KitchenAid Fresh Prep Slicer/Shredder attachment for KitchenAid Stand Mixers. All of these are faster, but more expensive, than the hand-operated grinders.

Techniques

Ella Szabó loved baking beautiful tortes and cakes like those served at the finest pastry shops and coffeehouses in Central Europe. Admittedly, some of those delicious treats take time to mix, bake, and decorate, requiring you to follow several steps to achieve the final product. But it's worth all that work in the kitchen, especially for a special occasion. And your family and friends will appreciate the effort you made to present them with such an elegant dessert.

Although the instructions for some of Ella's tortes look long on the page, once you learn the techniques for making tortes, you'll see how easy they really are. Here are several tips for ensuring that these recipes turn out successfully every time.

- **Pan preparation:** Torte and cake recipes require that you butter the inside of the baking pan(s), then dust them with flour to keep the batter from sticking to the pan while it bakes. (Sometimes the pans are also lined with baking parchment to prevent sticking.) Ella Szabó preferred to butter both the bottom and sides of her cake pans. Other professional cooks recommend buttering only the bottom, so the batter will cling to the sides of the pan as it bakes, helping it to rise higher. Use the technique that works best for you.

- **Measuring flours:** Although professional bakers always weigh the flour for their recipes, most American home cooks prefer to measure flour in cups and fractions of a cup. Lightly spoon wheat flour into a measuring cup and level off the top with a knife. Measure nut flour by spooning it into the correct-size measuring cup, gently tapping the side of the cup and smoothing over the top of the nut flour without pressing down on it. If a recipe specifies *firmly packed* nut flour, spoon it into the correct-size measuring cup and push down with the spoon to compress it as you fill the cup.

- **Beating/folding eggs:** Many torte recipes use egg yolks and egg whites beaten separately, with the fluffy whites then folded into the heavier egg-yolk mixture to lighten the batter and make it rise in the oven. It is easier to separate the yolks and whites when the eggs are cold from the refrigerator—but best to let the separated eggs then warm up to room temperature before beating them so the whites will whip up to a larger volume.

Always use a spotlessly clean large bowl (steel, copper, or glass, not plastic or aluminum) and clean beaters for beating the egg whites. Start beating them on low speed until they become foamy, then increase the mixer speed to medium-high and beat until the whites form soft mounds. (Some cooks add ¼ teaspoon of cream of tartar to stabilize the beaten whites.) If the recipe requires sugar to be added, gradually add it 1 tablespoon at a time while continuing to beat on medium-high speed.

Whether or not sugar is required, beat the egg whites until they form peaks when the beaters are lifted out of them. For many torte recipes, the whites are beaten until stiff peaks form, with the fluffy whites still looking glossy, not dry. If the whites appear dry and start forming clumps, they have been over-beaten and will not cause the batter to rise properly.

Home cooks often use a large rubber spatula for folding flour into a beaten egg-and-sugar mixture and for folding stiffly beaten egg

Whisks can be used to fold other ingredients into beaten egg whites.

whites into a batter. Many professional cooks recommend using a large balloon whisk (in the same way you'd use a rubber spatula) to incorporate more air into the mixture and eliminate any lumps without deflating the delicate batter.

To fold fluffy egg whites into a batter, start by gently stirring one-fourth of the beaten whites into the batter to lighten it. Then put the remaining whites on top of the batter and gently fold them into it, using a rubber spatula or balloon whisk. Quickly and gently spread the batter in the prepared baking pan and place it in the preheated oven, before the egg whites can deflate.

To fold dry ingredients into beaten eggs whites (wheat flour, nut flour, spices), carefully sprinkle the dry ingredients around the edges of the whites and gently fold them into the whites.

To combine both wet and dry ingredients with a beaten egg mixture such as egg yolks or whole eggs that have been beaten with sugar until creamy, add the other ingredients on top of the beaten egg mixture and stir, or fold, as indicated in the recipe.

Double boilers are used for making custard fillings for tortes.

- **Using a double boiler:** Some recipes require that certain ingredients (such as eggs, chocolate, or cream) be warmed before mixing with the other ingredients. Use a metal double boiler (not glass), because after heating the ingredients in the top part, you often need to set the top in a bowl of ice water for the mixture to cool a little before continuing with the recipe. (A glass double boiler might shatter from the sudden change of temperature.) If you don't have a double boiler, use a metal mixing bowl set on top of a saucepan of simmering water.

  The top of the double boiler should be set over, but not touching, the simmering water in the bottom part. Adjust the heat to keep the water only at a simmer, no hotter.

  If melting chocolate in the top of a double boiler, the pan should be set over water that is very hot but not simmering. Stir occasionally until no more lumps of chocolate remain.

- **Cake layers:** Some tortes are baked in one cake pan (usually a springform pan), then sliced horizontally into thinner layers so a filling can be added. Others are made with layers baked separately in more than one pan, then stacked together with a filling between them. And others are baked in a single thin layer, in an 11 × 17–inch rimmed baking sheet (or sheet pan), then cut into equal-size portions (usually three long strips) that are stacked in layers with a filling between them.

To slice a single cake layer horizontally into two thinner layers, use a long, serrated knife. Or use a long piece of thread or unflavored dental floss wrapped around the outside of the cake equidistant from the top and bottom. Cross both ends of the thread and pull it tightly around the cake to keep it from slipping, then continue pulling on it to make it slice through the cake, dividing the cake into equal-size layers. Or simply use a commercial cake leveler/slicer (see "Equipment" section).

- **Whipped cream:** Many of Ella's tortes are garnished with, or completely covered with, whipped cream. The whipped cream is often spread on the torte just before serving, but if it is put on the torte well in advance, the torte must be refrigerated, usually for at least 2 hours before serving. Whipped cream is also piped through a pastry bag fitted with a decorating tip, as a final flourish on several of her tortes.

Always use heaving whipping cream with at least 36% fat. The cream, the mixing bowl, and the metal beaters should all be very cold before the cream is whipped, so chill them in the freezer for about 20 minutes in advance. Beat the cream on medium-high speed until soft peaks form, then reduce the speed to medium and continue beating until stiff peaks form. Don't overbeat, or the cream will start solidifying into particles of butter.

Sweetening the whipped cream with confectioners' sugar will help to stabilize it, so it will hold its shape and not start melting if the cake or torte sits at room temperature for a long time (such as on a buffet table). Add the sugar and any other flavorings (such as vanilla extract) after the cream just begins to thicken while beating it. Some cooks add a small amount of cream of tartar, or a teaspoon of cornstarch, or even a tablespoon of instant vanilla pudding mix to the cream as a stabilizer. You can also use a commercial stabilizer, such as Whip It.

Many professional bakers stabilize their whipped cream by adding gelatin to it. For each 1 cup of cream to be whipped, use 1 teaspoon of unflavored gelatin sprinkled on top of 1½ tablespoons of cold water. Let the gelatin absorb the water, then melt that mixture in the microwave for about 5 seconds. Let it cool to barely lukewarm while you beat the cream on medium-high speed into soft peaks. Very slowly pour the melted gelatin into the cream while beating constantly on low speed.

Then increase the mixer speed to medium-high and continue beating until stiff peaks form. Use as directed in the recipe.

- **Keep cool!** At elegant pastry shops and coffeehouses in Hungary, fancy tortes and cakes are displayed in lighted, glass-fronted cool cases. Likewise, many of your home-baked tortes and cakes—especially those covered with whipped cream or a chocolate glaze—should be refrigerated until serving time. Cover them with a cake dome or very large mixing bowl to prevent absorption of any odors in the refrigerator. Then let them sit at room temperature, uncovered, for 15 minutes before serving. Keep any leftover portions refrigerated too.

Gluten-Free Tips

- **Pan preparation:** Use a gluten-free flour mixture or rice flour instead of wheat flour for buttering and flouring the inside of a baking pan, to prevent the batter from sticking to the pan.

  Some bakers dust their buttered pans with fine dry breadcrumbs instead of flour. To make a gluten-free substitute for breadcrumbs, put two large handfuls of unsweetened Rice Chex cereal into a gallon plastic bag, press out as much of the air as you can, and seal the bag tightly. Crush the cereal into fine pieces with a rolling pin, then use those for dusting your baking pan. Commercial gluten-free bread crumbs are also available at major grocery stores and online.

- **Cake/torte batters:** For recipes that use only a small amount of ingredients that contain gluten—2 tablespoons of dry breadcrumbs, 2 to 4 tablespoons of wheat flour—you can usually substitute an equal amount of gluten-free breadcrumbs, or a commercial gluten-free flour (preferably one containing xanthan gum). But for recipes using a larger amount of dry breadcrumbs or wheat flour, one-to-one measurement substitutions are not recommended, because the texture of the cake or torte will be affected.

PART ONE

NUT-FLOUR TORTES AND ROULADES

ALMOND-FLOUR TORTES

► **NOTE:** In these recipes, volume measurements of *nut flours* (in cups) are an approximation, to the nearest fraction of a cup, based on grinding the amount of *whole nuts* listed in the recipe. Volume measurements of nut flours can vary slightly, depending on the size of the nuts and the method used for grinding them. Since hand-ground nut flours are fluffier and less dense than store-bought nut flours, the volume of hand-ground nut flour can be slightly larger than the volume of store-bought nut flour, even though they both weigh the same. Likewise, tortes made with commercially ground nut flours tend to be a bit denser than those made with nuts ground by hand.

For best results measure out the amount of *whole nuts* needed in a recipe (in cups, or by weight in ounces), then grind them in your own kitchen and use the amount of nut flour that you produce. If using *store-bought nut flour*, then use the number of cups of *nut flour* specified in the recipe.

Belli Tante's Apple Torte

This one-of-a-kind recipe created by Belli Tante has never been published before. A round torte, it has a delicate, vanilla-flavored almond-flour cake layer covered with slowly cooked grated apples and an apricot glaze topped with fluffy meringue and toasted slivered almonds. Following Belli Tante's wishes, I give the recipe as it appears in the original manuscript, so everyone can enjoy one of my all-time favorite tortes.

Cake base

2 sticks (16 tablespoons, 8 ounces, 1 cup) unsalted butter, at room temperature
¾ cup granulated sugar
5 large egg yolks
½ cup heavy whipping cream or half-and-half
1½ tablespoons pure vanilla extract
½ cup all-purpose flour
1 teaspoon baking powder
2 cups unblanched almond flour (made from about 6½ ounces or 1¼ cups whole almonds)

Apple layer

5 Granny Smith apples (2 pounds)
Finely grated zest of 1 lemon

Meringue layer

3 large egg whites, at room temperature
1 cup granulated sugar

Assembly

1 cup apricot jam
½ cup (2 ounces) lightly toasted slivered almonds

▶ Preheat the oven to 325°F. Line the bottom of a 10-inch-diameter round springform pan with parchment paper. Butter and flour the paper and all sides of the pan, shaking out the excess flour.

▶ **Cake base:** In the bowl of a stand mixer fitted with the paddle attachment, beat the butter and sugar on high speed until the mixture is light in color and texture, about 3 minutes. Beat in the egg yolks one at a time until well blended, then beat until very light, about 1 minute longer. Mix the cream and vanilla in another bowl and add to the butter mixture, beating for about 1 minute.

- In a separate bowl, whisk the all-purpose flour together with the baking powder. Add the almond flour. Combine the flour mixture with the butter mixture and beat at medium speed until well combined. Press the dough into the prepared pan in an even layer.

- Bake on the middle rack of the oven at preheated 325°F for 20 minutes. Then turn the oven down to 300°F and bake about 15 minutes more, until the cake is firm when lightly pressed on the top. Transfer the cake to a wire rack and cool completely in the springform pan. This base of the torte can be made a day ahead, kept in the pan, and refrigerated, or it can be tightly sealed in a plastic freezer bag and frozen for up to three months.

▶ **Apple layer:** Peel and core the apples. Coarsely grate them and place in a colander. Let the colander stand in the sink or a bowl for 30 minutes. (Don't worry about the apples discoloring. When baked they will form a beige-colored, jam-like layer.) Then squeeze out the juices with your hands. Place the apples in a medium saucepan. Cook over medium heat, stirring constantly, until the apples have softened and all moisture has evaporated, about 10 minutes. Add the lemon zest. Cool completely.

▶ **Meringue layer:** Using a handheld mixer at high speed, beat the egg whites in a medium bowl until soft peaks form. Gradually add the sugar until stiff peaks form that are still glossy, not dry.

▶ **Assembly:** If the base of this torte has been frozen, bring to room temperature and place back in the 10-inch springform pan before proceeding with torte assembly. Preheat the oven to 200°F.

42

- Heat the apricot jam in a small saucepan over low heat until melted, about 2 minutes. Spread the jam evenly over the baked torte layer. Cover the jam evenly with the apple mixture. Top this evenly with meringue, or put the meringue in a pastry bag and, using a large round or star tip, pipe the meringue to cover the whole top of the torte. Sprinkle the slivered almonds over the meringue, or stick them into the meringue mounds.

- Bake the assembled torte on the middle rack of the oven at 200°F for about 40–50 minutes, so the meringue will dry from the inside out. Remove from the oven.

- Position the broiler rack about 8 inches from the source of the heat and preheat the broiler. Then put the torte under the broiler for 30 seconds to 1 minute, watching carefully to avoid burning, until the meringue is lightly toasted on top. (Or use a kitchen blowtorch to lightly brown the meringue.)

- Cool completely in the pan set on a wire rack. Refrigerate for about 4 hours, then remove the sides of the pan. Carefully slide a large spatula under the cake to remove it from the parchment paper and transfer it to a serving plate. Cut into wedges to serve. Keep any leftovers in the refrigerator.

▶ Makes 8 to 10 servings.

Belli Tante's Apple Torte with meringue topping.

HUNGARIAN APPLES

As a major agricultural country in the heart of Europe, Hungary has long been known for its production of apples, which often constituted up to 60 percent of all fruits grown there. In addition to the apple trees lovingly tended in many people's gardens, there are also large commercial orchards in several parts of Hungary, where the sandy soil is especially good for apple cultivation. The largest apple-growing region is in northeastern Hungary, in Szabolcs-Szatmár-Bereg County and the two adjacent counties.

Many varieties of apples are grown in Hungary, including Golden Delicious, Idared, Jonathan, Jonagold, Gala, Granny Smith, and numerous heritage types of old cultivars. Hand-picked from late summer until well into autumn, apples are eaten fresh; stored in cool places throughout the winter; cooked in cakes, tortes, strudels, fritters, puddings, and sweet soups; pressed into apple juice; and distilled into clear apple brandy.

Thirty years ago, Hungary was the most important exporter of apples in Europe, especially of apple juice in concentrated form. But climate change, competition from other countries such as China, and other economic factors have reduced Hungarian apple production and exports in this century. However, Hungarians themselves still enjoy munching on a good, crisp apple, sipping a glass of aromatic apple brandy, and seeing acres of orchards filled with pink-and-white apple blossoms in spring.[3]

Editor

Sári Fedák's Chestnut-Almond Torte

This torte is named for a much-loved star of the Hungarian theater who was also the wife of Ferenc Molnár, the well-known Hungarian playwright. Famous all over Europe, from Budapest to Berlin, Paris, and London, Sári Fedák even performed in America, too, and often played the men's role in operettas. She was a contemporary of Belli Tante, and they moved in the same social circles in Hungary. Sári Fedák enjoyed entertaining people from all walks of life, so it's appropriate that a special Hungarian torte bears her name.

Cake layers

½ cup (5 ounces weight) canned, unsweetened chestnut puree
5 egg yolks
1½ sticks (12 tablespoons, 6 ounces, ¾ cup) unsalted butter, at room temperature
½ cup confectioners' sugar
½ teaspoon pure vanilla extract
⅔ cup unblanched almond flour (made from about 2½ ounces or ½ cup almonds)
⅓ cup plus 1 tablespoon all-purpose flour
1 teaspoon baking powder
3 ounces semi-sweet chocolate, grated
7 large egg whites, at room temperature

Filling

2 cups heavy whipping cream, very cold
¼ cup confectioners' sugar
½ cup (5 ounces weight) canned, unsweetened chestnut puree
3 tablespoons dark rum

Garnish

2 ounces semi-sweet chocolate

▶ Preheat the oven to 325°F. Line the bottom of a round, 9-inch-diameter springform pan with parchment paper. Butter the bottom and the sides of the pan, sprinkle with flour, and shake out the excess flour.

▶ **Cake layers:** In the bowl of a stand mixer with the paddle attachment, beat the egg yolks and chestnut puree at medium speed until no lumps remain. Add the butter, sugar, and vanilla, beating until well combined.

- In another bowl combine the nut flour, all-purpose flour, baking powder, and grated chocolate. Add this to the chestnut-butter mixture, stirring to mix well.

- In a separate bowl, beat the egg whites on high speed with a whisk attachment until stiff, glossy peaks form.

- With the stand mixer on low speed, add about one-third of the egg whites to the chestnut mixture to lighten the batter. Then use a rubber spatula to gradually fold in the rest of the egg whites until well incorporated. Pour this batter into the prepared springform pan, spreading it evenly with a spatula.

- Bake on the middle rack of the oven at 325°F for 30 minutes, or until the top feels firm to the touch. Let the cake cool in the pan set on a wire rack.

▶ **Filling:** Chill a mixing bowl and a mixer whisk attachment in the freezer. Whip the cream to soft peaks in the chilled bowl, gradually adding the confectioners' sugar. Beat until stiff peaks form.

- In a separate bowl mix together the chestnut puree and dark rum until well combined. Fold in 1 cup of the whipped cream to lighten the mixture. Refrigerate the rest of the whipped cream.

▶ **Assembly:** Remove the cake from the pan and carefully cut it in half horizontally. Put one layer on a serving platter. Spread the chestnut-rum mixture evenly on that layer, then place the other cake layer on top. (You can make this torte up to this point a day in advance. Cover with plastic wrap and refrigerate until needed.)

▶ **Garnish:** Just before serving, spread the remaining whipped cream on the top and sides of the torte. Use a vegetable peeler to make chocolate curls to cover the top of the torte or grate the chocolate over the top.

▶ Makes 8 servings.

CHESTNUT PUREES

Chestnuts are a well-loved ingredient in Hungarian cooking, especially for sweet dishes: cakes, tortes, puddings, ice cream. Sweetened chestnut puree, flavored with vanilla and rum and topped with whipped cream, is a popular dessert in Hungary and many other European countries.

Purists insist on making chestnut puree from scratch— a laborious process that requires removing the nuts' spiky, hedgehog-like outer husk, then removing the brown papery shell and the bitter inner skin before simmering the starchy nuts in water or milk until tender. The softened chestnuts are finally put through a sieve or potato ricer, and sugar is added if the puree is to be used for desserts. But most Hungarians today just purchase commercially made chestnut puree, sweetened or unsweetened, sold in cans or in small foil-wrapped boxes in the freezer section of their local supermarket. Hungarian sweetened chestnut puree in boxes is also flavored with rum and vanilla. It has a firmer texture than sweetened chestnut spreads, and home cooks sometimes just slice it into slabs and garnish it with whipped cream for a quick and easy dessert.

Good-quality canned French chestnut puree is available in the United States from the Clément Faugier company. Its Chestnut Spread (Crème de Marrons de L'Ardèche), flavored with sugar and vanilla and sold in a distinctive Art Nouveau–style can, is a seductively tasting soft spread that can be used as a cake batter ingredient or a cake filling, or slathered on pancakes, or spooned over ice cream. (Some people just eat it straight from the can!) A firmer sweetened chestnut puree sold in cans is Hero Gastronomique Vermicelle

Dessert / Chestnut Puree. For other recipes, sweet or savory, it is better to use firmer, unsweetened chestnut puree, sold by Faugier as Purée de Marrons, because the cook can control the amount of sugar and other flavorings to add, as well as the texture of the puree, for use in those recipes.

Editor

Almond Meringue Torte with Coffee-Cream Filling

This heavenly pastry combines crisp almond meringue with a delicious mocha-cream filling. A family heirloom from the turn of the century, the recipe came to me from the collection of a dear friend's mother. It's well worth the time it takes to make, especially when you see the delight of your guests and hear their appreciative "oohs and aahs."

Meringue layers

2¼ cups toasted almond flour (made from about 7½ ounces or
    1½ cups blanched almonds)
1 cup confectioners' sugar
1 cup egg whites (from about 6 large eggs), at room temperature
Pinch of salt

Filling

4 egg yolks
3 tablespoons granulated sugar
¼ cup espresso coffee (decaffeinated can be used)
1½ sticks (12 tablespoons, 6 ounces, ¾ cup) unsalted butter, at
    room temperature

Garnish

1 cup slivered blanched almonds, toasted and coarsely chopped

► Preheat the oven to 275°F. On a piece of parchment paper, draw three parallel rectangles, each 14 inches long and 3 inches wide, leaving about ¾ inch between them. Turn the paper over and place it on a lightly buttered 11 × 17–inch baking sheet.

► **Meringue layers:** Whisk together the almond flour and confectioners' sugar in a medium bowl. In the bowl of a stand mixer fitted with the whisk attachment, beat the egg whites with a pinch of salt on medium speed until stiff peaks form that are still glossy, not dry. Gradually fold in the almond-sugar mixture until well blended.

- Spoon one-third of the meringue mixture into a pastry bag fitted with a ⅓-inch plain (round) piping tip. Fill in one of the rectangles on the parchment paper by piping the meringue onto it, starting from the inside edge of the rectangle. Repeat for the next two rectangles. Smooth the top of each. If you are not comfortable using a pastry bag, you can use a large spoon to spread the meringue mixture evenly on each rectangle.

- Bake on the middle rack of the oven at 275°F for 45 to 60 minutes, until the meringue is firm to the touch and the color of light toast. Slide the parchment paper with the meringues onto a wire rack to cool completely.

▶ **Filling:** Whisk the egg yolks and sugar together in a bowl. Gradually add the espresso coffee. Pour this mixture through a sieve into the top of a metal double boiler, set over, but not touching, simmering water. Cook, stirring constantly, for about 5 minutes, until the mixture thickens. Take the pan off the heat. Remove the top of the double boiler and set it in a bowl filled with 2 inches of ice water to stop the cooking.

- In the bowl of a stand mixer fitted with the paddle attachment, beat the butter until light and fluffy. Gradually add the coffee-egg mixture, slowly beating until well blended. Refrigerate for 1 hour, until firm.

▶ **Assembly:** Carefully peel the parchment paper off the meringues. Place one layer, flat side down, on a large serving platter. Spread one-fourth of the mocha-cream filling on this layer and repeat with the next layer, using one-fourth of the filling. Top with the third layer, flat side up, then cover the top and sides of the torte with the remaining mocha cream, smoothing it with a spatula.

▶ **Garnish:** Sprinkle the chopped almonds on the top and sides of the torte. Cover loosely with plastic wrap. Refrigerate overnight to allow the flavors to meld. The texture of this torte will be chewy but not soft.

▶ Makes 12 to 14 servings.

Esterházy Torte

Classic Esterházy Torte is composed of several thin layers of baked, nutty meringue (dacquoise)—*made with walnuts, almonds, or hazelnuts— alternating with layers of rich, boozy buttercream. The top layer of crunchy* dacquoise *is spread with apricot jam and then covered with white fondant. Toasted almond pieces are pressed onto the sides, and the white fondant on top is decorated with a chocolate spider-web design. Ella's somewhat simpler recipe features five layers of almond* dacquoise, *vanilla buttercream custard for the filling and the icing, almonds on the sides, and sweetened whipped cream served as a garnish.*

Editor

▶ **NOTE:** This recipe requires advance preparation, as well as the use of five 9-inch-diameter round springform pans. If you don't have that many in your kitchen, borrow some extras from friends.

Filling

1½ cups milk, at room temperature
¼ cup cornstarch
½ cup granulated sugar
6 egg yolks
Pinch of salt
3 sticks (24 tablespoons, 12 ounces, 1½ cups) unsalted butter, cut into small pieces
¼ cup pure vanilla extract

Cake layers

10 large egg whites, at room temperature
Pinch of salt
1¼ cups granulated sugar
3¼ cups almond flour (made from about 12 ounces or 2½ cups whole unblanched almonds)
Scant ½ cup all-purpose flour

Garnish

1 cup blanched and toasted almonds (your choice of slivered, flaked, or chopped almonds)
1 cup heavy whipping cream, very cold
3 tablespoons confectioners' sugar

▶ **Filling:** Whisk the milk and cornstarch together in a mixing bowl. Add the egg yolks, sugar, and salt, whisking until well blended.

- Pour this mixture through a sieve into the top of a metal double boiler, set over, but not touching, simmering water. Stir vigorously until the mixture starts to thicken and sticks to the spoon. Remove the pan from the heat, then set the top of the double boiler in a bowl of ice water. Keep stirring while adding the butter pieces, until well blended. Beat this mixture with a handheld mixer until it cools down, about 4 minutes, then stir in the vanilla, cover, and refrigerate for 3 hours.

▶ **Cake layers:** Preheat the oven to 325°F. Line the bottom of five 9-inch-diameter round springform pans with parchment paper. Butter the paper and the sides of the pans. Sprinkle with flour, shaking out the excess.

- In the bowl of a stand mixer fitted with the whisk attachment, beat the egg whites with a pinch of salt at medium speed until soft peaks form. Continue to beat, gradually adding the sugar until stiff peaks form that are still glossy, not dry.

- In another bowl whisk the almond flour together with the all-purpose flour. Carefully fold the egg whites into the flour mixture until they are well incorporated.

- Divide the batter evenly among the five baking pans, gently spreading it into an even layer in each pan. Bake on the middle rack of the oven at 325°F for 15 minutes, two or three pans at a time on the oven rack. Turn off the heat and let the cake pans sit in the oven for an additional 5 minutes. The baked batter should have a lightly toasted color. Remove the pans from the oven and set on a wire rack to cool.

▶ **Assembly:** Place a 12-inch doily on a cake platter. Peel the parchment paper off one cake layer and place that layer on top of the doily. Spread one-sixth of the vanilla-cream filling on top of the cake layer, then

52

peel the paper off the next cake layer and place that layer on top of the vanilla cream. Spread that layer with one-sixth of the vanilla cream mixture. Repeat with the next two cake layers, placing the fifth cake layer on top. Then cover the top and sides of the torte with the remaining filling. Refrigerate the torte overnight.

► **Garnish:** Press toasted almonds (slivered, flaked, or chopped) onto the sides of the torte. Chill a mixing bowl and a mixer's whisk attachment in the freezer. Whip the cream on medium-high speed in the chilled bowl until soft peaks form, then gradually add the confectioners' sugar while beating until stiff peaks form.

• Serve slices of the torte with dollops of the whipped cream.

► Makes 8 to 10 servings.

A PRINCELY TORTE

An elegant example of the baker's art, Classic Esterházy Torte was invented in Budapest in the late nineteenth century and supposedly named for Prince Pál Antal Esterházy de Galántha (Paul III Anton, Prince Esterházy, in English), a very wealthy Hungarian aristocrat, diplomat, and politician who lived from 1786 to 1866. The richness of this torte reflects the vast riches of the Esterházy family, members of the Hungarian nobility who owned several castles and palaces. For thirty years during the eighteenth century, Franz Joseph Haydn was the court musician (composer and conductor) at the beautiful Rococo Esterházy castle in Fertőd, Hungary (fashioned after Louis XIV's palace at Versailles). A hundred years later, the elaborate Esterházy Torte was created and became one of the most famous cakes in Central Europe. It was sold in most of the pastry shops and coffeehouses in Budapest and Vienna, as it still is today.[4]

Editor

Sour-Cherry Torte

You can make this tasty torte a day in advance and refrigerate it overnight. Assemble and decorate with whipped cream just before serving.

Cake layers

6 large eggs, at room temperature

5 tablespoons granulated sugar

2 cups almond flour (made from about 6½ ounces or 1¼ cups unblanched almonds)

Finely grated zest of 2 lemons

1 cup sun-dried, pitted sour cherries, soaked in 2 tablespoons of rum for 2 hours or overnight*

*Canned or fresh cherries can also be used (pitted, washed, and drained before soaking in rum)

Filling

2 cups heavy whipping cream, very cold

¼ cup confectioners' sugar

▶ Preheat the oven to 350°F. Line the bottom of an 8-inch-diameter round springform pan with parchment paper. Butter the paper and the sides of the pan. Sprinkle with flour, shaking off the excess.

▶ Cake layers: In the bowl of a stand mixer fitted with a whisk attachment, beat the eggs and sugar together at high speed for about 10 minutes, until light and fluffy. In another bowl whisk together the almond flour and the lemon zest, then gradually fold this mixture into the egg-sugar mixture. Pour half of this batter into the prepared pan.

• Drain the excess rum from the cherries in a sieve. Place the cherries on top of the cake batter in the pan, then pour the remaining batter on top.

• Bake on the middle rack of the oven at 350°F for about 20 to 25 minutes, or until torte feels firm to the touch. Cool completely in the pan set on a wire rack. Then release and remove the sides of the pan and transfer the cake to a serving platter.

► **Filling:** Chill a mixing bowl and a mixer's whisk attachment in the freezer. Whip the cream on medium-high speed in the chilled bowl until soft peaks form, then gradually add the confectioners' sugar while beating until stiff peaks form.

► **Assembly:** Using a long, serrated knife, cut the torte horizontally 1 inch down from the top to prevent the cherries from being disturbed. Spread ⅓ cup of whipped cream on top of the remaining cake, then return the cut-off part of the cake to its position on top. Cover the top and sides of the cake with whipped cream. (For a fancier presentation, use a pastry bag fitted with a large star nozzle to pipe the whipped cream onto the cake.)

► Makes 8 to 10 servings.

HUNGARIAN CHERRIES

Cherries have been cultivated in Hungary since the Middle Ages. Today several varieties, both sweet and sour, are grown there, both by individuals in backyard gardens and by companies that own large commercial orchards. Hungary is now one of the largest producers of cherries in the European Union and the largest exporter of sour cherries in Europe. No wonder that cherries are second only to apples as a commercial fruit crop in Hungary.[5]

Harvested in June and July, cherries make their way onto Hungarian tables in many forms: fresh, for eating straight from the tree; pressed into juice; cooked into jellies and jams; and baked into cookies, cakes, pies, tartes, and strudels. Whole cherries, preserved in sugar syrup flavored with cinnamon, cloves, and rum, are also a tasty topping for puddings, pancakes, and frozen desserts.

An especially popular dish in Hungary is chilled cherry soup, a pretty pink concoction made with sour cherries, sugar, and red wine, garnished with sweet or sour cream, and served either as a first course or a dessert. Cherries are also made into a sweet after-dinner liqueur and distilled, along with their pits, into a clear, potent, aromatic fruit brandy.

Hungarian confectioners are well known for their boozy, chocolate-covered cherries. Whole cherries are first macerated in liquor, usually brandy, for two to three months. After being drained and pitted, they are dipped in a sugar fondant that is allowed to dry before being coated with semi-sweet chocolate. As the chocolate dries, the inner layer of solid fondant begins to combine with some of the brandy that oozes out of the cherries, producing the richly flavored sweet liquid that bursts from the chocolate shell when you bite into it. Individually wrapped in gold-colored foil and packaged in fancy boxes, these delicious Hungarian confections are enjoyed year-round, and especially at Christmastime.[6]

Editor

Chocolate-Almond Torte
with Apricot Glaze

Chocolate and almonds have always been a favorite pair in the culinary world. But their natural flavors are often masked by too much sugar. Here, their luxury blends together into a velvety texture enhanced by the subtle presence of an apricot glaze.

Cake base

6 large eggs, at room temperature
1¼ cups confectioners' sugar
1 stick (8 tablespoons, 4 ounces, ½ cup) unsalted butter, at room temperature
3 ounces semi-sweet chocolate, grated
3 cups almond flour (made from about 10½ ounces or 2 cups whole unblanched almonds)
1 tablespoon baking powder

Apricot glaze

¾ cup apricot jam
1 tablespoon sugar

Whipped cream

1 cup heavy whipping cream, very cold
2 tablespoons confectioners' sugar

▶ Preheat the oven to 300°F. Butter a 9-inch-diameter round springform pan and line the bottom with parchment paper. Butter and flour the paper and all sides of the pan, shaking out the excess flour.

▶ **Cake base:** In the bowl of a stand mixer fitted with the whisk attachment, beat the egg yolks with the sugar at high speed until thick, about 10 minutes. The mixture will resemble whipped heavy cream. Add the butter, a little at a time, and beat until it is fully incorporated and smooth. Add the chocolate and beat for 1 minute more.

- In another bowl beat the egg whites until stiff peaks form. Fold the beaten egg whites into the egg-sugar mixture.

- In a separate bowl, whisk together the almond flour and baking powder. Carefully fold this into the egg mixture until the ingredients are evenly distributed, but don't overmix the ingredients. It is okay if the batter is still a bit lumpy. Spread the batter evenly in the pan.

- Bake on the middle rack of the oven for 20 minutes at 300°F, then increase the temperature to 325°F and bake for an additional 35 minutes, or until a toothpick inserted in the center comes out clean. Cool completely in the pan set on a wire rack. Then remove the torte from the baking pan and transfer it to a cake plate.

▶ **Apricot glaze:** Place the jam and sugar in a small saucepan over low heat. Using a wooden spoon, stir constantly for a few minutes, or until the mixture is smooth.

▶ **Whipped cream:** Chill a mixing bowl and a mixer's whisk attachment in the freezer. Whip the cream on medium-high speed in the chilled bowl until soft peaks form, then gradually add the confectioners' sugar while beating until stiff peaks form.

▶ **Assembly:** Cover the top of the cake with apricot glaze. (The cake can be frozen at this point for up to three months in a tightly sealed freezer bag. Bring it to room temperature about 2 hours before serving.)

- Cover the sides of the torte with some of the whipped cream. Spoon the remaining whipped cream into a pastry bag fitted with a large star tip and pipe rosettes along the top edge of the torte. Cut into wedges for serving.

▶ Makes 8 to 10 servings.

Chocolate-Almond Torte with Buttercream Filling

This is an example of a more complicated Chocolate-Almond Torte, made in the shape of a long rectangle, with layers of rich buttercream.

Cake layers

10 large eggs, at room temperature
½ cup plus 1 tablespoon granulated sugar
3 ounces semi-sweet chocolate, grated
2½ cups almond flour (made from about 9½ ounces or 1¾ cups of unblanched almonds)
2 tablespoons all-purpose flour

Filling

8 egg yolks, at room temperature
½ cup milk, at room temperature
½ cup granulated sugar
5 ounces semi-sweet chocolate, grated
1 stick (8 tablespoons, 4 ounces, ½ cup) unsalted butter, at room temperature

Whipped cream

2 cups heavy whipping cream, very cold
¼ cup confectioners' sugar

Garnish

2 ounces semi-sweet chocolate, grated

▶ Preheat the oven to 325°F. Line the bottom of an 11 × 17–inch rimmed baking sheet with parchment paper. Butter the paper and sides of the pan. Sprinkle with flour, shaking off the excess.

▶ **Cake layers:** In a *6-quart bowl* of a stand mixer fitted with the whisk attachment, beat the eggs and sugar at high speed for about 10 minutes, until light and fluffy. In a separate bowl, whisk together the chocolate, almond flour, and all-purpose flour. Use a flexible spatula to fold the flour mixture into the egg-sugar mixture.

- Spread the batter evenly in the prepared pan. Bake on the middle rack of the oven at 325°F for 15–20 minutes, or until the top feels firm to the touch. Let the cake cool in the pan set on a wire rack.

▶ **Filling:** In a small bowl, lightly whisk together the egg yolks and milk. Pour through a sieve into the top of a metal double boiler set over, but not touching, simmering water. Add the granulated sugar. Cook, stirring constantly, until the mixture is thick, about 6 minutes. Remove the top of the double boiler and set it in a bowl filled with 2 inches of ice water to stop the cooking. Stir the egg-custard mixture until lukewarm.

- In a separate bowl, beat the butter until light and fluffy. Add the grated chocolate, then stir this mixture into the egg custard until well blended. Refrigerate for 1 hour.

▶ **Assembly:** Based on your serving platter size, select the size of the torte that best fits your needs.

Option 1: Cut the cake layer into three long strips, each 17 inches long and about 3½ inches wide.

Option 2: Cut the cake layer into three long strips, each 11 inches long and 5½ inches wide.

- Remove one layer from the parchment paper and place on a long serving platter. Spread one-third of the filling evenly on top of that layer, then place another cake layer on top of it. Spread with one-third of the filling, then cover with the top cake layer. Trim the short ends to even out the edges, and trim the long sides, too, if necessary. Spread the remaining filling on the sides of the torte. Refrigerate for a few hours or overnight.

▶ **Whipped cream:** Chill a mixing bowl and mixer whisk attachment in the freezer. Whip the cream in the chilled bowl until soft peaks form, then gradually add the confectioners' sugar. Beat until stiff peaks form.

▶ **Garnish:** Spread the top of the torte with some of the whipped cream. Fill a pastry bag with the remaining whipped cream, and use the star tip to make small rosettes around the top edge and the bottom edge of the torte. Sprinkle the top with the grated chocolate.

▶ Makes 10 to 16 servings, depending on length of torte.

Caramelized-Almond Cream Torte

Several Hungarian tortes are made in this long, thin shape. If you don't have a serving platter long enough, make one from a piece of heavy cardboard, about 20 inches long and 8 inches wide, covered with aluminum foil.

Cake layers

10 egg whites, at room temperature
Pinch of salt
1 cup confectioners' sugar
3 cups almond flour (made from about 10½ ounces or 2 cups blanched almonds)

Caramelized-almond flour

¾ cup granulated sugar
1¼ cups (6 ounces) toasted blanched almonds

Filling

1½ sticks (12 tablespoons, 6 ounces, ¾ cup) unsalted butter, at room temperature
2 tablespoons granulated sugar
5 egg yolks, at room temperature
1 cup milk, at room temperature
2 tablespoons all-purpose flour

Garnish

2 cups heavy whipping cream, very cold
¼ cup confectioners' sugar

▶ Preheat the oven to 300°F. Line the bottom of an 11 × 17–inch rimmed baking sheet with parchment paper. Butter the paper and sprinkle with flour, shaking off the excess.

▶ **Cake layers:** In the bowl of a stand mixer fitted with a whisk attachment, beat the egg whites with a pinch of salt until soft peaks form. Continue to beat, gradually adding the confectioners' sugar until stiff peaks form that are still glossy, not dry. Carefully fold in the almond flour until well combined.

- Spread this batter evenly on the prepared baking sheet and bake in the preheated 300°F oven for 12 to 15 minutes, until the top feels firm to the touch. Set on a wire rack to cool.

▶ **Caramelized-almond flour:** Heavily butter or oil an 11 × 17–inch rimmed baking sheet. Melt the sugar in a heavy-bottom saucepan over medium heat, stirring constantly, until it turns a golden caramel color. Working quickly, add the toasted almonds, stirring until well coated. Pour this on the prepared pan, being careful not to touch it because the mixture is very hot. Let it cool completely, then break it up with your hands. Grind this into flour in your nut grinder or food processor. Set aside about ⅓ cup for the garnish. The remaining caramelized almond flour will be used for the filling.

▶ **Filling:** In the bowl of a stand mixer fitted with the paddle attachment, beat the butter and sugar until light and fluffy. Set aside.

- In another bowl whisk together the egg yolks, milk, and flour. Pour this mixture through a sieve into the top of a metal double boiler set over, but not touching, simmering water. Cook, stirring constantly, until the mixture thickens. Remove the pan from the heat, then take the top pan off the double boiler and set it in a bowl or pan containing 2 inches of ice water to stop the cooking. Stir the mixture until lukewarm. Gradually add this custard to the bowl with the butter-sugar mixture. Then add the caramelized almond flour, mixing it slowly. Refrigerate at least 2 hours to firm up.

▶ **Assembly:** Based on your serving platter size, select the size of torte that best fits your needs.

Option 1: Cut the cake layer into three long strips, each 17 inches long and about 3½ inches wide.

Option 2: Cut the cake layer into three long strips, each 11 inches long and 5½ inches wide.

- Place one layer on a serving platter. Spread one-third of the filling evenly on one layer of the cake. Top with another layer of cake and one-third of the filling, then repeat with the last layer. Trim the short ends to even out the edges and the long sides if necessary. (The torte may be prepared a day ahead to this point and refrigerated.)

▶ **Garnish:** Chill a mixing bowl and mixer whisk attachment in the freezer. Whip the cream to soft peaks in the chilled bowl, gradually adding the sugar. Beat until stiff peaks form. Spread the whipped cream on the sides of the torte and score the sides of the cake, horizontally, with a cake comb. Sprinkle the top evenly with the remaining ⅓ cup of caramelized almond flour.

▶ Makes 12 to 16 servings.

FROM ALMONDS TO MARZIPAN

Almonds, which probably originated in China, came to Europe from the Middle East, where almond trees have been grown since ancient times. Early Greeks and Phoenicians planted almond trees around the Mediterranean region, and later the Arabs expanded almond orchards, and introduced sugar-cane cultivation, in the areas they conquered and colonized in Spain, Sicily, and Malta.

During the Middle Ages, merchants in ports like Venice and Genoa shipped almonds to central and northern Europe, including Hungary, since most of those countries were too far north for successful almond cultivation on their own soils. But almonds were such a tasty and versatile nut that they became an ingredient in many dishes, both sweet and savory.

In Hungary today almonds are used mainly in cakes, cookies, and confections. Finely ground almonds are essential for making many of Hungary's elegant tortes, and almonds—chopped, slivered, flaked—decorate many Hungarian desserts.

A much-loved confection in Hungary is marzipan, a smooth paste of finely ground, blanched sweet almonds mixed with sugar (and sometimes other ingredients such as egg whites, honey, almond extract, a small amount of bitter almonds, rosewater, or orange blossom water) and kneaded into a pliable dough. Marzipan originated in the Middle East and spread to northern Europe from Venice and the eastern Mediterranean during the time of the Crusades, from the eleventh through thirteenth centuries. By the 1400s marzipan was known in Hungary, where (as in other parts of northern Europe) the costly confection became a favorite of the wealthy upper classes, whose cooks molded it into elaborate and fantastic shapes for use as showy centerpieces on banquet tables and edible finales to medieval feasts.

Today, Budapest is one of Europe's centers of marzipan manufacture, even though there are only a few small almond orchards in Hungary itself. Local confectioners coat marzipan with chocolate and wrap marzipan around pieces of dried apricots soaked in apricot brandy, or dried plums macerated in plum brandy. They craft the malleable marzipan mass into miniature fruits, vegetables, and animal figurines, tinted with edible colors, and shape it into lifelike flowers as decorations for cakes. Marzipan is also rolled out into sheets to use as fillings or coverings for fancy cakes and pastries.

Hungarians love their marzipan so much that marzipan museums have been created in several Hungarian cities. One of the most popular is the Szabó-Szamos Marzipan Museum in Szentendre, a pleasant (but now rather touristy) artists' village near Budapest. Originally established by two of Hungary's most famous confectioners, the small museum features displays of colorful marzipan shaped into Disney characters, a Cinderella coach, a massive wedding cake, a cactus garden, a detailed replica of the Hungarian parliament building, and even life-size effigies of Michael Jackson and Princess Diana of Wales. Demonstrations of marzipan making are offered in a traditional confectionery kitchen, and the adjacent café and pastry shop sells a wide variety of luscious Hungarian cakes, tortes, ice creams, and marzipan candies.[7]

Editor

Orange-Almond Torte

This is another example of the kind of torte that can be made a day ahead of time, refrigerated until needed, and then garnished just before serving.

Candied orange peel

2 large oranges
1 cup water
10 tablespoons of granulated sugar

Cake layers

8 large eggs, at room temperature
½ cup plus 1 tablespoon granulated sugar
1¾ cups unblanched almond flour (made from about 6½ ounces
   or 1¼ cups almonds)
2 tablespoons finely crumbled dry white bread crumbs
3 tablespoons all-purpose flour
2 tablespoons freshly squeezed orange juice
1 tablespoon freshly squeezed lemon juice

Filling

2 egg yolks
2 tablespoons water
1¼ cups freshly squeezed orange juice (from approximately 3
   oranges)
¼ cup granulated sugar
¼ cup all-purpose flour
2 sticks (16 tablespoons, 8 ounces, 1 cup) unsalted butter
3 tablespoons Mandarine Napoléon or Grand Marnier liqueur

Garnish

2 cups heavy whipping cream, very cold
¼ cup confectioners' sugar
Candied orange peel

▶ **Candied orange peel:** Wash the oranges and dry thoroughly. Use a vegetable peeler to remove strips of peel, avoiding the bitter white pith. Put the orange peel into a small saucepan with 1 cup of water and the 10 tablespoons of sugar. Bring the mixture to a boil and continue boiling for about 10 minutes, to make a heavy syrup. Remove pan from the heat and let cool, then remove the orange peel from the syrup and finely chop it.

▶ Preheat the oven to 350°F. Line the bottom of a 9-inch-diameter round springform pan with parchment paper. Butter the paper and all sides of the pan. Sprinkle with flour and shake off the excess.

▶ **Cake layers:** In a *6-quart bowl* of a stand mixer fitted with the whisk attachment, beat the eggs and sugar at high speed for about 10 minutes until light and fluffy. In another bowl whisk together the almond flour, bread crumbs, and all-purpose flour, then gradually fold this mixture into the eggs. Fold in the orange and lemon juice. Pour this mixture into the prepared springform pan.

- Bake on the middle rack of the oven for 30 minutes at 350°F until the top feels firm to the touch. Cool completely in the pan set on a wire rack.

▶ **Filling:** Whisk together the egg yolks and water in a small bowl. Pour this mixture through a sieve into the top of a metal double boiler. Add the orange juice, sugar, and all-purpose flour. Place the double boiler over, but not touching, simmering water. Cook, stirring constantly, until the mixture thickens. Remove the pan from the heat and set the top of the double boiler in a bowl containing 2 inches of ice water to stop the cooking. Stir the custard to help it cool.

- In another bowl beat the butter until light and fluffy. Add the cooled custard, 3 tablespoons of the candied orange peel (from recipe above), and the orange liqueur, mixing well. Cover and refrigerate until firm.

▶ **Assembly:** Use a long, serrated knife to cut the cake into three evenly-sized layers. Spread about one-fourth of the filling on that bottom layer, then put another layer on top of it, spread with one-fourth of the filling. Place the final layer on top and spread the remaining filling on the top and sides of the torte. (The torte may be made a day ahead to this point and refrigerated.)

▶ **Garnish:** Chill a mixing bowl and mixer whisk attachment in the freezer. Whip the cream to soft peaks in the chilled bowl, gradually adding the sugar. Beat until stiff peaks form. Cover the top of the torte with whipped cream (and save the remaining whipped cream to serve with individual slices of the torte). Sprinkle the remaining candied orange peel on top of the torte. Refrigerate any leftovers.

▶ Makes 8 to 10 servings.

Coffee-Almond Torte

I was thrilled when my soon-to-be son-in-law asked me to bake a torte for the wedding rehearsal dinner. He chose this Coffee-Almond Torte with its distinctive flavor. The beautifully decorated torte not only looked good but also tasted divine. When my grandsons, Russell and later Spencer, were born, I happily made this delicious torte again, to celebrate their arrivals.

Cake layers

9 large egg whites, at room temperature
1 cup confectioners' sugar
2 cups toasted almond flour (made from about 6½ ounces or 1¼ cups toasted unblanched almonds)

Filling

1½ tablespoons powdered instant coffee (decaffeinated can be used)
6 tablespoons strong-brewed espresso coffee (decaffeinated can be used)
9 egg yolks
1 cup confectioners' sugar
3 sticks (24 tablespoons, 12 ounces, 1½ cups) unsalted butter, at room temperature, cut into several pieces

Garnish

1 cup of toasted blanched almonds (slivered or flaked), coarsely chopped

▶ Preheat the oven to 325°F. Line the bottom of an 11 × 17–inch rimmed baking sheet with parchment paper. Butter the paper and the sides of pan, then coat with flour, shaking out the excess.

▶ **Cake layers:** Using a stand mixer fitted with the whisk attachment, beat the egg whites until soft peaks form, then very slowly add the sugar. Beat until the egg whites are stiff but still glossy, not dry. Gently fold in the almond flour.

- Spread this batter evenly in the prepared pan. Bake on the middle rack of the preheated oven at 325°F for 10 minutes. Turn the heat up to 350°F and bake for another 5 minutes. Remove the pan from the oven and place it on a wire rack to cool completely.

▶ **Filling:** Dissolve the instant coffee in the espresso. Set aside.

- Whisk together the egg yolks, confectioners' sugar, and coffee mixture in the top of a metal double boiler. Set the pan over, but not touching, simmering water. Cook, stirring constantly, until mixture thickens, about 8 minutes. Remove the pan from the heat, then place the top of the double boiler in a bowl filled with 2 inches of ice water to stop the cooking. Stir the mixture until it is lukewarm, then add butter, stirring until completely incorporated.

▶ **Assembly:** Based on your serving platter size, select the size of torte that best fits your needs.

Option 1: Cut the cake layer into three long strips, each 17 inches long and about 3½ inches wide.

Option 2: Cut the cake layer into three long strips, each 11 inches long and 5½ inches wide.

- Place one layer on a long serving platter. Spread one-fourth of the coffee-cream filling on that bottom layer. Place another cake layer on top of that and spread with one-fourth of the filling. Add the last cake layer, then cover the top and sides with the remaining filling.

▶ **Garnish:** Cover the sides of the torte with the chopped almonds. Refrigerate for a few hours before serving.

▶ Makes 10 to 16 servings, depending on length of torte.

Chauncey Howell's Torte

I created this torte to honor Chauncey Howell, who hosted a radio talk show on station WGCH in Greenwich, Connecticut, in 1992. I was asked to be his sidekick on the show, and each time I was on the radio we talked about Hungarian food and pastries. I often brought in my newly baked tortes, too, which we would eat with gusto and discuss during the interview on the air. I must say that I had the time of my life! I still miss Chauncey Howell on ABC's Channel 7 in New York, where he was a funny man with a bow tie and a great big smile. He always reminded me that laughter is the best medicine in life.

Cake layers

10 large eggs, at room temperature
9 tablespoons granulated sugar
2½ cups of almond flour (made from about 9½ ounces or 1¾ cups of whole blanched almonds)

Filling

1½ cups confectioners' sugar
2 sticks (16 tablespoons, 8 ounces, 1 cup) unsalted butter, at room temperature
2½ cups almond flour (made from about 9½ ounces or 1¾ cups of whole blanched, toasted almonds)
¾ cup whole milk, at room temperature

Garnish

2 cups heavy whipping cream, very cold
¼ cup confectioners' sugar

▶ Preheat the oven to 325°F. Line the bottom of an 11 × 17–inch rimmed baking sheet with parchment paper. Butter the paper and sprinkle with flour, shaking off the excess.

▶ **Cake layers:** In a *6-quart bowl* of a stand mixer fitted with the whisk attachment, beat the eggs and the sugar at high speed for about 10 minutes, until light and fluffy. Gradually fold in the almond flour. Spread the cake batter evenly in the prepared pan, smoothing over the top.

- Bake on the middle rack of the oven at 325°F for 20 to 25 minutes, or until the cake feels firm to the to touch. Let the cake cool in the pan set on a wire rack.

▶ **Filling:** In the bowl of a stand mixer fitted with the paddle attachment, beat the butter and sugar until light and fluffy. Gradually add the almond flour and milk, beating until well incorporated. Refrigerate for an hour to firm up.

▶ **Assembly:** Based on your serving platter size, select the size of torte that best fits your needs.

Option 1: Cut the cake layer into three long strips, each 17 inches long and about 3½ inches wide.

Option 2: Cut the cake layer into three long strips, each 11 inches long and 5½ inches wide.

- Place one layer on a long serving platter. Spread about one-fourth of the filling evenly on top of one strip of cake and stack the next layer on top of that. Spread one-fourth of the filling evenly on that layer, then place the third layer on top. Trim the short ends to even them out and trim the long sides if necessary. Cover and smooth out the top and sides with the remaining filling.

▶ **Garnish:** Chill a mixing bowl and the mixer whisk attachment in the freezer. Whip the cream in the chilled bowl to soft peaks, gradually adding the sugar. Beat until stiff peaks form.

- Serve the torte with a dollop of whipped cream on each slice.

▶ Makes 10 to 16 servings, depending on length of torte.

HAZELNUT-FLOUR TORTES

▶ **NOTE:** In these recipes, volume measurements of *nut flours* (in cups) are an approximation, to the nearest fraction of a cup, based on grinding the amount of *whole nuts* listed in the recipe. Volume measurements of nut flours can vary slightly, depending on the size of the nuts and the method used for grinding them. Since hand-ground nut flours are fluffier and less dense than store-bought nut flours, the volume of hand-ground nut flour can be slightly larger than the volume of store-bought nut flour, even though they both weigh the same. Likewise, tortes made with commercially ground nut flours tend to be a bit denser than those made with nuts ground by hand.

For best results measure out the amount of *whole nuts* needed in a recipe (in cups, or by weight in ounces), then grind them in your own kitchen and use the amount of nut flour that you produce. If using *store-bought nut flour*, then use the number of cups of *nut flour* specified in the recipe.

Isabella Torte

In Hungary it's the custom for people to celebrate their "name day" every year instead of the actual date of their birth. All Hungarian first names are listed on the yearly calendar on a certain date (always on the same date, year after year), hence that date is your name day. On that day you are expected to receive well-wishers, friends, and relatives who show up at your door to wish you a happy name day. No gifts are given to the celebrant, but a bouquet of flowers is appropriate. Guests also bring pastries, tortes, and drinks to add to the occasion. For one of these happy name day celebrations—Isabella's name day, July 12—Belli Tante's friend Herzi, who was an accomplished and creative home baker, developed this torte and named it in her honor, since Belli Tante's real first name was Isabella.

Cake layers

9 large egg whites, at room temperature
1 cup confectioners' sugar
3¼ cups toasted hazelnut flour (made from about 12 ounces or 2½ cups whole toasted and skinned hazelnuts)

Filling

1 cup milk, at room temperature
4 large egg yolks
2 tablespoons cornstarch
1 cup granulated sugar
4 ounces bittersweet chocolate, grated
2 sticks (16 tablespoons, 8 ounces, 1 cup) unsalted butter, at room temperature

▶ Preheat the oven to 325°F. Line the bottom of an 11 × 17–inch rimmed baking sheet with parchment paper. Butter the paper and sides of the pan. Sprinkle with flour, shaking off the excess.

▶ **Cake layers:** In the bowl of a stand mixer fitted with a whisk attachment, beat the egg whites until soft peaks form. Continue to beat, gradually adding the sugar, until stiff peaks form that are still glossy, not dry. Gently fold in the hazelnut flour until well combined.

- Spread the batter evenly in the prepared baking pan. Bake on the middle rack of the oven at 325°F for 15 to 18 minutes, until the top is firm and golden brown. Let the cake cool in the pan placed on a wire rack.

▶ **Filling:** Lightly whisk together the milk, egg yolks, cornstarch, and sugar in the top of a metal double boiler. Place over, but not touching, simmering water. Cook, stirring constantly, until the mixture thickens, about 8 minutes. Take the pan off the heat. Remove the top of the double boiler and set it in a bowl of ice water to stop the cooking. Stir in the chocolate. Using a handheld mixer on low speed, add the room-temperature butter to the egg-chocolate mixture, beating to combine well. Refrigerate for 2 hours.

▶ **Assembly:** Based on your serving platter size, select the size of torte that best fits your needs.

Option 1: Cut the cake layer into three long strips, each 17 inches long and about 3½ inches wide.

Option 2: Cut the cake layer into three long strips, each 11 inches long and 5½ inches wide.

- Place one layer on a long serving platter. Spread one-fourth of the chocolate-buttercream filling on that bottom layer. Place another cake layer on top of that and spread with one-fourth of the filling. Add the last cake layer, then trim the short ends and the long sides if necessary to even out the edges. Cover the top and sides with the remaining chocolate buttercream.

- To serve, slice crosswise with a serrated knife into 1- to 1½-inch-thick slices.

▶ Makes 10 to 16 servings, depending on length of torte.

Caramelized-Hazelnut Torte

Belli Tante's circle of friends included a Hungarian who had married a Baltic Russian noble émigré, Baron Stephanoh Düsterlohe, thus becoming the Baroness Valeria "Wally" Düsterlohe. The baroness was both a great beauty and a talented baker in her own kitchen. In creating this torte, she enhanced her hazelnut flour by grinding the nuts with caramelized sugar and also added a touch of framboise (raspberry eau-de-vie) to her chocolate glaze. The recipe for this torte has never been published before, but no longer shall it remain unknown. Just remember to handle the hot caramelized sugar carefully; it can cause serious burns.

Caramelized-hazelnut flour

1 cup granulated sugar
1 cup toasted and skinned hazelnuts, (about 4½ ounces)

Cake

6 large egg whites, at room temperature
Pinch of salt
3 tablespoons granulated sugar
1 tablespoon pure vanilla extract
3 tablespoons all-purpose flour
1 teaspoon baking powder
1 cup toasted hazelnut flour (made from about 4½ ounces or a
    generous ¾ cup of toasted and skinned hazelnuts)
Caramelized hazelnut flour (from recipe above)

Chocolate glaze

2½ tablespoons unsalted butter, at room temperature
2 tablespoons light corn syrup
5 ounces semi-sweet chocolate, grated or finely chopped
1 tablespoon framboise (raspberry liqueur) or light rum (optional)
25 toasted and skinned hazelnuts for decoration

Garnish

1 cup heavy whipping cream, very cold
2 tablespoons confectioners' sugar

▶ Preheat the oven to 325°F. Line the bottom of a 9-inch-diameter round springform pan with parchment paper. Butter the paper and all sides of the pan. Sprinkle with flour, shaking off the excess.

▶ **Caramelized-hazelnut flour:** Oil or butter an 11 × 17–inch rimmed baking sheet. Heat 1 cup of sugar in a medium-size, heavy-bottom saucepan over medium-low heat, stirring constantly with a wooden spoon until it caramelizes to a golden-brown color. Working quickly, stir in the toasted hazelnuts. Avoid touching the sugar, as it is very hot and can cause severe burns. Pour the sugared nuts onto the well-oiled baking pan. Cool completely, then grind them into flour using a nut grinder or food processor.

▶ **Cake:** In the bowl of a stand mixer fitted with the whisk attachment, beat the egg whites with a pinch of salt at medium speed until soft peaks form. Add the sugar, one tablespoon at a time, then beat on high speed until stiff peaks form that are still glossy, not dry. Fold in the vanilla.

● In a separate bowl, whisk together the all-purpose flour, baking powder, hazelnut flour, and caramelized hazelnut flour. Carefully fold this mixture into the egg whites, blending thoroughly.

● Pour the batter into the prepared pan and bake on the middle rack of the oven at 325°F for 30 minutes, or until a light golden color. The cake is done when a toothpick inserted in the middle comes out clean.

● Let the cake cool in the pan set on a wire rack. When the cake has completely cooled, run a knife around the edges of the pan and remove the sides of the pan. Carefully invert the cake onto a plate and peel the parchment paper off the bottom. Then invert the cake onto a serving platter. (At this point the cake can be wrapped tightly in plastic wrap and frozen until needed. Thaw before glazing with chocolate.)

▶ **Chocolate glaze:** Melt the butter with the corn syrup in a small saucepan over low heat, stirring constantly. When well combined, remove from the heat. Gradually stir in the chocolate, stirring until very smooth. Set aside to cool to lukewarm. Stir in the framboise or rum.

- Cover the cake with the chocolate glaze and "crown" it with the 25 whole hazelnuts by placing them, evenly spaced, in a single row around the top circumference of the cake. Once the torte is glazed, you can serve it immediately, or you can refrigerate it until time to garnish and serve.

▶ **Garnish:** Chill a mixing bowl and mixer whisk attachment in the freezer. Whip the cream to soft peaks in the chilled bowl, gradually adding the sugar. Beat until stiff peak forms.

- To serve, slice the torte into wedges and serve with dollops of whipped cream on the side.

▶ Makes 8 to 10 servings.

HAZELNUTS

Small brown nuts rich in protein, hazelnuts date back several thousand years as a food source in Europe. Also known in English as filberts and cobnuts, they grow on bushy trees that thrive in the cooler climates of the planet's northern temperate zone. Turkey is the largest producer and exporter of hazelnuts today, followed by Italy, where hazelnuts are used in making the popular chocolate-hazelnut spread Nutella, as well as the sweet hazelnut liqueur Frangelico.[8]

Hazelnuts figure prominently in Hungarian cake and pastry making. In a 2002 article about hazelnuts published in the *Greenwich Time*, a Connecticut newspaper, Ella Szabó recalled that when she was a child in Hungary, her family's orchard "featured hazelnut bushes planted as a hedge around the perimeter of the property." She went on to write, "In Hungary, hazelnuts were recognized at the turn of the [twentieth] century for their fine texture and taste. Roasted hazelnuts were ground into a flour to replace wheat flour, giving the resulting tortes and pastries added flavor and a light texture. This technique, which was developed by famous pastry chefs, became so well known that roasted hazelnut flour was used in households throughout Hungary. When used in a cream frosting, the unique taste and texture lend an element of the exotic."[9]

Editor

Emperor's Torte

Although she named it the Emperor's Torte, Belli Tante's recipe for this simpler homemade version of the famous Imperial Torte is very different from the classic Viennese creation. Hers is round instead of square, made with hazelnut flour instead of almonds, uses no marzipan, and is covered with sweetened whipped cream instead of milk chocolate. Despite those considerable differences, it's still a delicious torte!

Editor

Cake layers

8 large eggs, at room temperature

7 tablespoons granulated sugar

2 cups plus 1 tablespoon toasted hazelnut flour (made from about 8 ounces or 1¾ cups toasted, skinned hazelnuts)

3 ounces semi-sweet chocolate, grated

1 tablespoon finely ground espresso beans (about 8 to 10 beans; decaffeinated can be used)

Filling

3 large egg yolks

3 tablespoons milk

1 tablespoon cornstarch

1 stick (8 tablespoons, 4 ounces, ½ cup) unsalted butter, at room temperature

¼ cup granulated sugar

Garnish

2 cups heavy whipping cream, very cold

¼ cup granulated sugar

2 ounces coarsely chopped semi-sweet chocolate

▶ Preheat the oven to 325°F. Line the bottom of a 10-inch-diameter round springform pan with parchment paper. Butter the paper and sides of the pan. Sprinkle with flour and shake off the excess.

▶ **Cake layers:** In a *6-quart bowl* of a stand mixer fitted with the whisk attachment, beat the eggs and the sugar at high speed for about 10 minutes, until light and fluffy and the mixture resembles whipped cream.

- In a small bowl whisk together the hazelnut flour, grated chocolate, and ground espresso beans. Gradually fold this mixture into the egg mixture. Pour the batter into the prepared pan and bake on the middle rack of the oven at 325°F for 40 minutes, or until the top feels firm to the touch.

▶ **Filling:** In the top of a metal double boiler set over, but not touching, simmering water, whisk together the egg yolks, milk, and cornstarch. Cook, stirring constantly, until the mixture thickens, about 5 minutes. Take the pan off the heat. Set the top of the double boiler in a bowl with 2 inches of ice water to stop the cooking. Stir this custard mixture until it cools.

- Using a handheld mixer, beat the butter and sugar together in a medium bowl until the mixture is light and fluffy. Fold the custard into the butter mixture until well blended.

▶ **Assembly:** Remove the cake from the pan and carefully cut it horizontally into three even layers. Remove the parchment paper from the bottom and place that cake layer on a serving platter. Spread half of the filling evenly on that bottom layer. Add the second layer and spread the remaining filling evenly over it. Then put the third cake layer on top. Cover and refrigerate for a few hours or overnight.

▶ **Garnish:** Chill a mixing bowl and mixer whisk attachment in the freezer. Whip the cream in the chilled bowl until it forms soft peaks, gradually adding the sugar. Then beat until stiff peaks form. Refrigerate until needed.

- Just before serving, cover the top and sides of the cake with the whipped cream and cover the top evenly with the chopped chocolate. Any extra whipped cream can be served with each slice. Refrigerate leftover torte.

▶ Makes 8 to 10 servings.

IMPERIAL TORTE

In 1873, in anticipation of the World's Fair to be held in Vienna that year, a magnificent private palace in the central part of the city was converted into the grand Hotel Imperial. According to legend, the night before the hotel was to open, Xavier Loibner, a young apprentice in the hotel's kitchen, invented a special torte for the inaugural banquet to be held the next day, April 28. The honored guest was Franz Joseph I, emperor of the Austro-Hungarian Empire, along with many of his titled friends who had come to Vienna to attend the fair.

Apparently the emperor favored Loibner's rich-tasting, square-shaped, chocolate-and-almond torte over all the other desserts on offer that day. And with the emperor's imprimatur, a new Viennese treat, complete with its own legend, was born.

A century and a half later, the five-star Hotel Imperial is still welcoming guests, and its pastry chefs are still making the torte that pleased the emperor's palate. The original Imperial Torte consists of six layers of thin, delicate, crispy almond pastry alternating with layers of fluffy-light chocolate cream, the entire square torte wrapped in a blanket of almond marzipan, then covered with a smooth chocolate glaze.

The hotel's pastry chefs have also branched out to produce variations on the classic Imperial Torte. In 2006 they created a special Mozart Edition in honor of the 250th birthday of the Austrian composer Wolfgang Amadeus Mozart, made with pistachio marzipan and covered with a milk-chocolate glaze.

The two versions available today, in addition to the original Imperial Torte, are the Schwarze Orange (Dark Orange) variation, with coffee-scented chocolate cream, orange-flavored marzipan, and a dark chocolate glaze. The Feine Himbeere (Fine Raspberry) version incorporates raspberry paste into the basic recipe. Surely the old emperor would have approved of all of these elegant iterations of the original square chocolate-and-almond torte that captured his attention back in 1873.[10]

Editor

WALNUT-FLOUR TORTES

▶ **NOTE:** In these recipes, volume measurements of *nut flours* (in cups) are an approximation, to the nearest fraction of a cup, based on grinding the amount of *whole nuts* listed in the recipe. Volume measurements of nut flours can vary slightly, depending on the size of the nuts and the method used for grinding them. Since hand-ground nut flours are fluffier and less dense than store-bought nut flours, the volume of hand-ground nut flour can be slightly larger than the volume of store-bought nut flour, even though they both weigh the same. Likewise, tortes made with commercially ground nut flours tend to be a bit denser than those made with nuts ground by hand.

For best results measure out the amount of *whole nuts* needed in a recipe (in cups, or by weight in ounces), then grind them in your own kitchen and use the amount of nut flour that you produce. If using *store-bought nut flour*, then use the number of cups of *nut flour* specified in the recipe.

Handwritten recipe for Walnut Torte (in Hungarian)
by Ella's mother, Roza Kovács.

Walnut Torte with Walnut-Rum Filling

In Hungary every family had its own version of this torte. This is a fourth-generation recipe. Most families bought their nuts from the grocery store, but we had the good fortune of owning a small showcase orchard since my father was in the agricultural business. We had several walnut trees, one of them growing right in front of our cottage. My father built a bench around the trunk of that tree, and it shaded us from the hot days of summer and bore its fruits in the fall. When I think back to that time, I see myself and my sister, Roza, holding our little aprons to catch the falling walnuts while my father gently shook the branches. What fun we had! The walnuts had to be processed one by one and put into bins to dry—a tedious job indeed. My mother and grandmother ground the nuts by hand, just as I do, and used them for many kinds of pastries, strudels, and tortes. That's how I learned to love walnuts for their taste—and now I know how healthful they are, too.

Cake layers

10 large eggs, at room temperature
9 tablespoons granulated sugar
2 cups walnut flour (made from 7 ounces or 2 cups of walnut halves)

Filling

1 cup whole milk, at room temperature
1 large egg, at room temperature, lightly beaten
1 tablespoon all-purpose flour
2 cups walnut flour (made from 7 ounces or 2 cups of walnut halves)
1 stick (8 tablespoons, 4 ounces, ½ cup) unsalted butter cut into small pieces, at room temperature
½ cup granulated sugar
1 tablespoon plus 1 teaspoon dark rum

Garnish

½ cup chopped walnut pieces for decoration
2 cups heavy cream, chilled
¼ cup confectioners' sugar

▶ Preheat the oven to 325°F. Line the bottom of an 11 × 17–inch rimmed baking sheet with parchment paper. Butter the paper and sides of the pan. Sprinkle with flour, shaking off the excess.

▶ **Cake layers:** In a *6-quart bowl* of a stand mixer fitted with the whisk attachment, beat the eggs and sugar together at high speed for about 20 minutes, until light and fluffy. The mixture will resemble whipped cream.

- Fold the walnut flour into the mixture using the whisk attachment from your mixer. Blend thoroughly, without deflating.

- Pour the batter into the prepared pan, spreading it evenly with a spatula. The baking sheet will be very full; the sponge will rise slightly during baking and deflate when cool. Bake on the middle rack of the oven at 325°F for 20 minutes, or until the top feels firm to the touch. Let the cake cool in the pan set on a wire rack.

▶ **Filling:** Pour the milk into the top of a metal double boiler set over, but not touching, simmering water. Heat the milk for about 3 minutes to lukewarm. Remove from heat.

- Place the egg and flour in a separate medium bowl. Slowly pour half of the warm milk into the egg, whisking until combined. Add this to the rest of the milk in the top of the double boiler by pouring it through a sieve to avoid lumps. Whisk constantly over medium heat until the mixture thickens to a custard consistency. Remove the pan from the heat and set the top of the double boiler in a bowl with 2 inches of ice water to stop the cooking. Stir the mixture until lukewarm. Add the walnut flour to the cooled custard. Set aside.

- In a medium mixing bowl, beat the butter and sugar together well for 4 minutes, until light and fluffy. Slowly add the rum and beat for 1 more minute. Fold the walnut custard into the butter mixture with a spatula, mixing until well incorporated. Refrigerate for 1 hour before using the filling.

▶ **Assembly:** Based on your serving platter size, select the size of torte that best fits your needs.

Option 1: Cut the cake layer into three long strips, each 17 inches long and about 3½ inches wide.

Option 2: Cut the cake layer into three long strips, each 11 inches long and 5½ inches wide.

- Place one cake strip on a long serving platter. Spread one-fourth of the walnut-rum filling evenly on one cake layer. Add the next cake layer on top of that, and spread one-fourth of the filling on it. Then top with the third cake layer. Trim the short ends to even out the edges and trim the long sides if necessary. Cover the top and sides with the remaining filling. Refrigerate at least 2 hours.

▶ **Garnish:** Chill a large mixing bowl and mixer whisk attachment in the freezer. Whip the cream to soft peaks in the chilled bowl, gradually adding confectioners' sugar. Beat until stiff peaks form.

- Remove torte from the refrigerator. Sprinkle chopped walnuts on top. Cover the sides of the torte with whipped cream. Using a star tip on a pastry bag filled with the whipped cream, pipe rosettes around the top and bottom edges of the cake. Serve immediately or refrigerate for a few hours, removing 30 minutes before serving.

▶ **NOTE:** You can wrap the refrigerated torte, without the whipped cream, in plastic wrap or place in a freezer bag and freeze for up to two months.

▶ Makes 10 to 16 servings, depending on length of torte.

Beatrix Torte

The recipe for this chocolate-walnut torte garnished with almond praline was provided by Peter Varga, proprietor of the Royal Corvin Mátyás Restaurant in Budapest, Hungary, where this torte was created. Surely the torte was named for Queen Beatrix, who was twice the queen of Hungary—first, through her marriage to King Matthias Corvinus of Hungary in 1476, and later to King Vladislaus II of Bohemia and Hungary in 1491.

Cake layers

8 large eggs, at room temperature
7 tablespoons granulated sugar
1 cup plus 1 tablespoon walnut flour (made from 3 ounces or
    1 cup of walnut halves)
¼ cup all-purpose flour
¼ teaspoon baking powder

Filling

2 cups whole milk, at room temperature
¾ cup granulated sugar
⅓ cup cornstarch
7 large egg yolks
1 cup cocoa powder (not Dutch process)
½ stick (4 tablespoons, 2 ounces, ¼ cup) unsalted butter cut into
    small pieces, at room temperature

Caramelized almonds

1¾ cup granulated sugar
1 cup toasted slivered almonds

▶ Preheat the oven to 325°F. Line the bottom of an 11 × 17–inch rimmed baking sheet with parchment paper. Butter the paper and sides of the pan. Sprinkle with flour, shaking off the excess.

▶ **Cake layers:** In a *6-quart bowl* of a stand mixer fitted with the whisk attachment, beat the eggs and sugar together at high speed for about

10 minutes, until light and fluffy. The mixture will resemble whipped cream.

- In a small bowl whisk together the walnut flour, all-purpose flour, and baking powder. Gradually fold the flour mixture into the egg mixture.

- Pour the batter into the prepared pan, spreading it evenly with a spatula. Bake on the middle rack of the oven at 325°F for 15 to 20 minutes, or until the top feels firm to the touch. Let the cake cool in the pan set on a wire rack.

▶ **Filling:** Pour the milk into the top of a double boiler set over, but not touching, simmering water. While the milk is warming, whisk the sugar and cornstarch together in a medium bowl. Add the egg yolks and beat together with the sugar and cornstarch until they turn pale yellow. Slowly pour half of the warm milk into the yolk mixture, whisking until combined. Add this to the rest of the milk in the top of the double boiler and continue to cook over simmering water, whisking constantly, until the mixture thickens. Stir in the cocoa powder. When well combined, gradually add the butter pieces, stirring until melted. Remove the pan from the heat and set the top of the double boiler in a bowl with 2 inches of ice water to stop the cooking. Stir the mixture until lukewarm, then cover and refrigerate for 1 hour.

▶ **Assembly:** Based on your serving platter size, select the size of torte that best fits your needs.

Option 1: Cut the cake layer into three long strips, each 17 inches long and about 3½ inches wide.

Option 2: Cut the cake layer into three long strips, each 11 inches long and 5½ inches wide.

- Place one strip of cake on a long serving platter. Spread one-fourth of the cocoa-custard buttercream on that layer. Add the next cake layer on top, and spread with one-fourth of the buttercream. Top with the third cake layer. Trim the short ends to even out the edges and trim the long sides if necessary. Cover the top and sides of the torte with the remaining buttercream filling. Cover loosely with plastic wrap and refrigerate at least 3 hours or overnight.

▶ **Caramelized almonds:** Oil or heavily butter a shallow metal baking pan or rimmed baking sheet. Heat the sugar in a medium-size, heavy-bottom saucepan over medium-low heat, stirring constantly, until it caramelizes to a golden-brown color. Add the toasted slivered almonds and toss lightly with a wooden spoon. Avoid touching the sugar; it is very hot and can cause severe burns. Pour the sugared nuts into the well-oiled baking pan. Cool completely, about 1 hour.

- Just before serving the torte, break up the caramelized almonds into small pieces and cover the top of the torte with them.

▶ Makes 10 to 16 servings, depending on length of torte.

WALNUTS

Walnuts grow in many temperate parts of the world, including Hungary, where large plantations of walnuts produce thousands of pounds each year, many of which are consumed domestically. Hungarian walnuts are also exported to France, Germany, and Great Britain. Historically, walnuts have long been used for culinary purposes (nutmeats, nut flour, nut oil), for making brown dyes for fabrics and dark ink for writing (from their shells), and for making furniture and tools (from the trees' wood).[11]

As Ella Szabó wrote in a newspaper article about Hungarian walnuts for the *Greenwich Time* newspaper in 2002, "In Hungary, walnuts are the most important nut in the pastry repertoire. Walnut flours are used in Hungarian desserts, cookies, and tortes. The most important item in the Hungarian household is the Dió Daráló, the [hand-operated metal] walnut grinder. When nut flour is substituted for wheat flours, baked goods come out lighter and tastier. At the turn of the [twentieth] century, famous pastry chefs and talented housewives created walnut flour pastries galore."[12]

Editor

Chocolate-Orange Torte

This torte is a family favorite. The orange zest in the sponge and Grand Marnier in the filling gives a heavenly, light orange essence to this torte. Use a gluten-free substitute (such as rice flour) in preparing the pan for baking, to make it fully gluten free.

Cake layers

8 large eggs, at room temperature
7 tablespoons granulated sugar
2½ cups walnut flour (made from about 8¾ ounces or 2½ cups walnut halves)
Finely grated zest of 1 large orange

Filling

5 ounces semi-sweet chocolate, grated or finely chopped
1½ cups milk, at room temperature
3 large egg yolks
2 tablespoons cornstarch
2 sticks (16 tablespoons, 8 ounces, 1 cup) unsalted butter, at room temperature
½ cup granulated sugar

Garnish

1 cup heavy whipping cream, very cold
2 tablespoons confectioners' sugar
2 tablespoons Grand Marnier (or other orange liqueur)
2 ounces semi-sweet chocolate, grated

▶ Preheat the oven to 325°F. Line the bottom of a 11 × 17–inch rimmed baking pan with parchment paper. Butter the paper and sides of the pan. Sprinkle with flour, shaking off the excess.

▶ **Cake layers:** In a *6-quart bowl* of a stand mixer fitted with the whisk attachment, beat the eggs and sugar at high speed for about 10 minutes until light and fluffy. The mixture will resemble whipped cream. Gently fold in the walnut flour and grated orange zest.

- Pour the batter into the prepared pan and smooth the top with a spatula. Bake on the middle rack of the oven at 325°F for 15 to 20 minutes. The cake is done when a toothpick inserted into it comes out nearly clean. Let the cake cool in the pan set on a wire rack.

▶ **Filling:** Place the chocolate and 1 tablespoon of water in the top pan of a double boiler and set aside. Bring the water in the double boiler to a boil, then turn off the heat and place the pan containing the chocolate over the hot water. Stir until the chocolate is melted, then remove the top pan and set aside, letting the chocolate cool to room temperature.

- Whisk milk, egg yolks, and cornstarch together in another bowl until well combined. Strain through a sieve into the top of a metal double boiler set over, but not touching, simmering water. Cook, stirring constantly, until the filling thickens, about 6 minutes. Set the top pan in a bowl of ice water to stop the cooking, and stir until lukewarm. Remove the pan from the water and use a hand mixer to beat in the melted chocolate.

- In the bowl of a stand mixer fitted with the paddle attachment, beat the butter and sugar on low speed for about 3 minutes, until light and fluffy. Gradually add the chocolate-custard mixture, beating on low speed until well blended. Cover and refrigerate for 1 hour.

▶ **Assembly:** Based on your serving platter size, select the size of torte that best fits your needs.

Option 1: Cut the cake layer into three long strips, each 17 inches long and about 3½ inches wide.

Option 2: Cut the cake layer into three long strips, each 11 inches long and 5½ inches wide.

- Place one layer on a long serving platter. Spread one-third of the filling evenly on that bottom cake layer. Top with the next cake layer and spread one-third of the filling on that. Top with the third cake layer. Trim the short ends to even out the edges and the long sides if necessary. Spread the remaining filling only on the sides of the torte. Let the cake rest a few hours or overnight.

▶ **Garnish:** Chill a mixing bowl and a mixer whisk attachment in the freezer. Whip the cream to soft peaks in the chilled bowl, gradually adding the confectioners' sugar and then adding the Grand Marnier. Beat until stiff peaks form.

- Spread the top of the torte with some of the whipped cream. Fill a star-tipped pastry bag with the remaining whipped cream and make small rosettes around the top and bottom edges of the torte. Sprinkle the top with the grated chocolate.

▶ Makes 10 to 16 servings, depending on length of torte.

One of Belli Tante's handwritten recipes (in German) for an orange-flavored torte.

Chocolate-Chestnut Torte

When I was a child walking home from school during the winter in Hungary, I would often see men roasting chestnuts over an open fire by the side of the street. We purchased the freshly roasted chestnuts to warm our hands and give us instant nourishment. Every household and pastry shop made a type of chestnut cake at Christmastime, and it was a tradition in our family to serve this beloved Chocolate-Chestnut Torte after Christmas Eve dinner. This special torte, an old family recipe, was a labor of love because the chestnuts had to be shelled, cooked, and pureed by hand. Today, chestnut puree (both sweetened and unsweetened) can be bought in cans—a real time saver for the baker.

Cake layers

10 large egg whites, at room temperature
1 teaspoon cold water
Pinch of salt
¾ cup granulated sugar
¼ cup all-purpose flour
½ cup walnut flour (made from about 1¾ ounces or ½ cup walnut halves)

Filling

7 ounces semi-sweet chocolate, grated or finely chopped
2 sticks (16 tablespoons, 8 ounces, 1 cup) unsalted butter, at room temperature
2 tablespoons confectioners' sugar
¼ cup dark rum
¼ teaspoon pure vanilla extract
2 cups unsweetened chestnut puree (20 ounces weight)

Garnish

2 cups heavy whipping cream, very cold
¼ cup confectioners' sugar

▶ Preheat the oven to 375°F. Line the bottom of an 11 × 17–inch rimmed baking sheet with parchment paper. Butter the paper and sides of the pan. Sprinkle with flour, shaking off the excess.

▶ **Cake layers:** In the bowl of a stand mixer fitted with the whisk attachment, beat the egg whites, water, and salt until soft peaks form. Continue to beat, gradually adding the sugar, until stiff peaks form that are still glossy, not dry. Whisk together the all-purpose flour and walnut flour in another bowl, then gently fold the flour mixture into the egg whites.

  • Spread the batter evenly in the prepared baking pan. Bake on the middle rack of the oven at 375°F for 12 to 15 minutes, until the top is firm and golden-brown. Let the cake cool in the pan set on a wire rack.

▶ **Filling:** Place the chocolate and 2 tablespoons of water in the top of a double boiler pan and set aside. Bring the water in the double boiler to a boil, then turn off the heat and place the pan containing the chocolate over the hot water. Stir until the chocolate is melted, then remove the top pan and set aside, letting the chocolate cool to room temperature.

  • Beat the butter and sugar together very well in a large mixing bowl, then slowly add the rum and vanilla. Beat until mixture is light and fluffy. Stir in the melted chocolate, and when the ingredients are well mixed, stir in the chestnut puree, mixing until well incorporated.

▶ **Assembly:** Based on your serving platter size, select the size of torte that best fits your needs.

Option 1: Cut the cake layer into three long strips, each 17 inches long and about 3½ inches wide.

Option 2: Cut the cake layer into three long strips, each 11 inches long and 5½ inches wide.

  • Place one cake strip on a long serving platter. Spread one-fourth of the chocolate-chestnut filling evenly on one cake layer. Add the next cake layer on top of that, and spread one-fourth of the filling on it. Then top with the third cake layer. Trim the short ends to even out the edges and trim the long sides if necessary. Cover the top and sides with the remaining filling. Refrigerate for a few hours before serving.

▶ **Garnish:** Chill a large mixing bowl and mixer whisk attachment in the freezer. Whip the cream to soft peaks in the chilled bowl, gradually adding confectioners' sugar. Beat until stiff peaks form.

- Cover the sides of the torte with whipped cream. Using a star tip on a pastry bag filled with the whipped cream, pipe a border around the top and bottom edges of the cake. Then use a plain tip to write the word "Chestnut" on the top.

▶ Makes 10 to 16 servings, depending on length of torte.

CHESTNUTS

Tall, beautiful chestnut trees spread their leafy branches throughout much of Europe, from England to Italy, from Portugal to Russia. In the autumn vendors selling fresh, roasted chestnuts make their appearance in European open-air markets and on street corners, remaining throughout the coldest days of winter. Chestnuts are especially associated with the Christmas–New Year season, when the smoky aroma and taste of roasted chestnuts, hot from the coals and wrapped in a paper cone, brighten up even the grayest, dreariest, or snowiest day.

Hungarians love chestnuts and eat them in many different forms, in both sweet and savory dishes. The Hungarian penchant for these tasty nuts is said to have begun when the Italian princess Beatrix of Naples married the Hungarian king Matthias Corvinus in 1476. Chestnuts were an important ingredient in Italy, and when Beatrix brought her Italian cooks and their recipes to the Hungarian royal court, capon stuffed with chestnuts became one of the king's favorite dishes. But surely Hungarian peasants had been eating chestnuts long before Beatrix arrived with her entourage of Italian chefs.

The versatile chestnut can be roasted, steamed, boiled, grilled, deep-fried, sautéed, pureed, pickled, candied, smoked, or dried. Chestnuts turn up on the table in soups and stews, sauces and gravies, fillings and stuffings, dumplings and pancakes, jams and marmalades, breads, cakes, cookies, tartes, tortes, puddings, and mousses. Sometimes they're mashed together with cream and butter and served as a starch on their own (like mashed potatoes), to accompany meat, poultry, or wild game such as pheasant, duck, boar, and venison. Sweetened chestnut puree garnished with whipped cream became a favorite dessert in Central Europe during the nineteenth century. And chestnuts can even be processed into sugar, milled into flour, and brewed into beer.

However, despite the Hungarians' demand for chestnuts, the country has never been a major producer of them. Because of soil conditions, Hungary has no large-scale plantations of chestnut trees like those of Italy, France, and Spain. The largest area of cultivated chestnuts is in the Trans-Danube region of southwestern Hungary, especially in the county of Zala. Most of the chestnuts eaten in Hungary today are imported from Italy.

But the influence of these nuts still shows up in the names of several Hungarian place names based on the Hungarian word for chestnut, *gesztenye*. Historical records show that chestnuts were among the foods traditionally eaten during the annual All Saints' Day observances in Hungary on November 1. And today chestnut festivals are held in the Hungarian towns of Keszthely, Iharosberény, and Velem during the nuts' harvest season in October.[13]

Editor

Judith's "Recovery Torte"

One day in 1938, Belli Tante's daughter, Judith, sat under the family cherry tree, feasting on the cherries in reach. She ended up in the hospital with terrible abdominal pains from a twisted intestine, and Belli Tante feared for her survival. Mrs. Müller, wife of the chief surgeon at the Veprőd hospital, kindly created this torte in celebration of Judith's recovery. The recipe was included in those that Belli Tante gave to me thirty years later.

Cake layers

¾ cup golden raisins
¼ cup dark rum
2 ounces semi-sweet chocolate, melted and still lukewarm
7 tablespoons granulated sugar
6 large egg yolks, at room temperature
2 cups walnut flour (made from about 7 ounces or 2 cups walnut
   halves)
10 large egg whites, at room temperature
Pinch of salt

Filling

2 ounces semi-sweet chocolate, cut into small pieces
1 cup milk, at room temperature
2 egg yolks
2 tablespoons all-purpose flour
6 tablespoons granulated sugar
2 tablespoons dark rum (from liquid reserved after soaking raisins)
2 sticks (16 tablespoons, 8 ounces, 1 cup) unsalted butter, at room
   temperature

▶ Line the bottom of a 10-inch-diameter round springform pan with parchment paper. Butter the paper and sides of the pan. Sprinkle with flour, shaking off the excess.

▶ **Cake layers:** Plump the raisins in the rum for 30 to 60 minutes, or cover and microwave for a few seconds. Set aside (do not drain off the rum yet). Melt the 2 ounces of chocolate for the cake batter in the top of a metal double boiler set over, but not touching, very hot water. Preheat the oven to 300°F.

- In the bowl of a stand mixer fitted with the paddle attachment, beat the 7 tablespoons of sugar and 6 egg yolks until light and fluffy. Stir in the lukewarm melted chocolate until no streaks remain, then fold in the ground walnuts. Drain the raisins and reserve the liquid. Fold the raisins into the egg-and-chocolate mixture.

- In another bowl of the stand mixer fitted with the whisk attachment, beat the 10 egg whites with a pinch of salt at high speed until stiff peaks form that are still glossy, not dry.

- Mix some of the egg whites into the egg-chocolate mixture to lighten it. Then gently fold in the rest of the egg whites.

- Pour the batter into the prepared pan, smoothing over the top. Bake on the middle rack of the oven at 300°F for 40 to 50 minutes until firm to the touch. Let the cake cool in the pan set on a wire rack.

▶ **Filling:** Melt the 2 ounces of chocolate for the filling in the top of a metal double boiler set over, but not touching, simmering water. Whisk the milk, 2 egg yolks, and flour together in a small bowl. Strain this into the melted chocolate. Cook over the simmering water, stirring constantly, until the mixture thickens. Remove the top of the double boiler and set it in a bowl with 2 inches of ice water to stop the cooking. Stir the mixture until lukewarm, then stir in the 6 tablespoons of sugar and the dark rum reserved from draining the raisins.

- In the bowl of a stand mixer fitted with the paddle attachment, beat the butter until light and fluffy. With the mixer on slow speed, add this chocolate mixture in a thin, steady stream until it is well blended with the butter. Cover and refrigerate until firm, at least an hour.

▶ **Assembly:** Remove the cooled cake layer from the pan and slice it in half horizontally. Peel off the parchment paper. Place the bottom half on a cake plate and spread one-third of the chocolate-cream filling evenly on top. Put the other layer on top, then cover the top and sides of the torte with the remaining filling.

▶ Makes 8 to 10 servings.

A slice of the deliciously restorative "Recovery Torte."

LABOR OF LOVE

To make a torte like this in the kitchen of a well-to-do Hungarian household during the first half of the twentieth century, the scene would have looked like this: A helper is bringing in a load of logs from the woodpile to start the fire in the big iron stove, so the oven will be warm enough by the time the cake is ready to bake. One person is beating the egg whites by hand with a large wire whisk in a copper bowl, for at least half an hour, while another person is beating the egg yolks in a separate bowl. Someone else is melting the chocolate on the stovetop. And another person is grinding the walnuts by hand. Fortunately, thanks to modern appliances, it takes much less work to make such a torte in today's kitchens!

Ella Szabó

Linzer Torte

My recipe for this classic Austrian torte won first place in a Bloomingdale's baking competition in New York. Later I made it for Ferenc Mádl, the former president of Hungary, when he visited the United States. He enjoyed it so much that he claimed it was the best Linzer Torte he had ever eaten. He also asked me to send the recipe to his wife so their whole family could enjoy it. Now you can taste it, too. The secret of this Linzer Torte is the use of finely ground walnuts and the jam made from seedless black raspberries (a special variety of raspberries). I use tart pans with scalloped edges because they make a more attractive torte than if you use plain round pans.

▶ NOTE: This recipe makes two tortes, with 8 servings each.

Pastry

3 cups all-purpose flour
4 teaspoons baking powder (preferably Rumford baking powder)
2½ cups walnut flour (made from about 8¾ ounces or 2½ cups walnut halves)
7 tablespoons granulated sugar
3 sticks (24 tablespoons, 12 ounces, 1½ cups) unsalted butter, at room temperature
2 large eggs, lightly beaten with a fork
Zest of 1 large lemon

Filling

1½ to 2 cups seedless black raspberry jam*

Garnish

Confectioners' sugar

*Editor's note: Ella Szabó always used a 20-ounce jar of McCutcheon's Black Raspberry Seedless Fruit Preserve (available online), which is very rich in taste. A jar of that weight holds 1½ cups of jam, or ¾ cup for each of

106

the two tortes. Use whatever berry jam or fruit preserve you choose, up to
1 cup for each Linzer torte.

▶ Preheat the oven to 350°F. Line the bottom of two 9-inch-diameter
tart pans or round springform pans with parchment paper. Butter the
paper and sides of the pans. Sprinkle lightly with flour, shaking off
the excess.

▶ **Pastry:** Whisk together the flour and baking powder in a large bowl.
Add the walnut flour and sugar, tossing the ingredients together lightly
with your fingers. Drop dabs of soft butter into the dry mixture. Mix
thoroughly with your fingers. Add the lightly beaten eggs and the lemon
zest. Knead lightly with your hands.

- On a well-floured piece of parchment paper, shape the dough by
hand into a thick log about 14 inches long. Wrap in plastic wrap and
refrigerate for 20 minutes, then put into the freezer for 20 minutes
(or just refrigerate it overnight).

- Cut the chilled log into four equal-length pieces. Two of these
pieces will be used for the torte bottoms and two for the latticework. Cut a ¾-inch piece crosswise off one log and place it on
the parchment-lined pan. Repeat this about six more times, spacing
the pieces evenly in the pan. Press them down with your fingers
to form an even surface of dough on the bottom and up the sides,
adding more pieces if necessary. Repeat this process for the second
prepared pan, using another log of dough.

▶ **Filling:** Spread half of the black raspberry jam evenly on top of the
dough in each pan.

▶ **Latticework top:** Cut ¾-inch pieces crosswise off another log, and cut
each of those pieces into half lengthwise (making two semicircles from
each piece). On a well-floured surface, use the palm of your hand to
roll each piece into a rope 9 inches long. When you complete the first
rope, lay it slightly off-center, across the jam-covered dough in one of
the pans. Then form seven more ropes in the same way, placing them
parallel and spaced evenly apart from the first rope. Cut or pinch off the
excess as the length across the pan gets smaller. Save the scraps to use in
the next step of the recipe. (For a different presentation, you can also roll

out the dough to a thickness of ⅛ inch and cut strips, ½ inch wide, with a fluted pastry cutter.)

- To complete the latticework, repeat the above process, laying the next eight ropes perpendicularly across the top of the ropes already in the pan.

Rolling dough for the latticework on top of a classic Linzer Torte.

- Make two long ropes from the remaining smaller ones (and the scraps), each rope long enough to go around the edge of each pan. Place one rope of dough around the inside perimeter of the pan, pinching the ends of the rope together to make a smooth circle. Lightly press this rope down to secure it to the ends of the lattice and to the pan.

- Bake on the middle rack of the oven at 350°F for 30 minutes, or until the pastry is lightly toasted in color. Remove the pan from the oven and set on a wire rack to cool completely. Then place it in the refrigerator for 3 hours to totally firm up (this helps in removing the parchment paper later).

- To remove the torte from the pan, carefully invert the torte onto a piece of wax paper dusted with confectioners' sugar. Remove the parchment paper, invert a serving platter or cake stand over the bottom of the torte, and carefully turn the torte and plate over together. (Or if you have a very large spatula, you can omit inverting the torte and just slide the spatula between the parchment paper and torte, then lift off the torte and place it on the serving platter.)

▶ **Garnish:** Sift confectioners' sugar lightly over the top. (You can also freeze this torte in a tightly sealed freezer bag for up to six months.)

▶ Makes two tortes (8 servings each).

LINZER TORTE

Named for the Austrian city of Linz on the Danube River, this torte is one of Austria's most well-known desserts, made in professional bakeries and home kitchens throughout the former Austro-Hungarian Empire, other German-speaking parts of Europe, and even far beyond. The Upper Austrian Provincial Museum in Linz holds the world's largest collection of historical Linzer Torte recipes. The earliest recorded recipe dates to a culinary manuscript of 1653, with the first printed recipe appearing in a cookbook in 1718. But since written or published recipes merely codify the ingredients and instructions for dishes that were already being made, this kind of torte is surely much older.

In today's terminology, this torte is actually a tart—a rather simple open-face pie with the crust on the bottom and a filling (in this case, fruit or berry jam) inside. But earlier recipes for Linzer Torte even included multilayered versions with various fruit fillings and baroque garnishes. And because the recipes' imported ingredients—almonds, sugar, spices—were very costly two hundred to three hundred years ago, the baking of Linzer Tortes was probably reserved for special occasions. Even now, Linzer Torte is often associated with winter holidays such as Christmas.[14]

Linzer Torte is one of those dishes where there are as many recipes for it as cooks who make it. The many variations made today include blanched or unblanched almonds, toasted hazelnuts, or walnuts in the crust (as in Ella Szabó's recipe), as well as different methods for making the crust; flavorings such as cocoa powder, cinnamon, cloves, cardamom, nutmeg, and lemon zest; and black currant, red currant, raspberry, strawberry, apricot, cherry, peach, or quince preserves for the filling.

Most Linzer Tortes are finished with a latticework top made of the same dough as the crust, sometimes cut with a scalloped pastry wheel for a fancier presentation. The latticework is also usually glazed with lightly beaten egg yolk or egg white and often garnished with granulated sugar, confectioners' sugar, or sliced almonds sprinkled over the top. Whether baked in a farmhouse kitchen or in an elegant pastry shop in Budapest or Vienna, Linzer Torte is a classic beloved by all.

Editor

Ella's version of Linzer Torte is easy to make.

TORTES WITH COMBINED NUT FLOURS

▶ **NOTE:** In these recipes, volume measurements of *nut flours* (in cups) are an approximation, to the nearest fraction of a cup, based on grinding the amount of *whole nuts* listed in the recipe. Volume measurements of nut flours can vary slightly, depending on the size of the nuts and the method used for grinding them. Since hand-ground nut flours are fluffier and less dense than store-bought nut flours, the volume of hand-ground nut flour can be slightly larger than the volume of store-bought nut flour, even though they both weigh the same. Likewise, tortes made with commercially ground nut flours tend to be a bit denser than those made with nuts ground by hand.

For best results measure out the amount of *whole nuts* needed in a recipe (in cups, or by weight in ounces), then grind them in your own kitchen and use the amount of nut flour that you produce. If using *store-bought nut flour*, then use the number of cups of *nut flour* specified in the recipe.

Budapest Torte

This easy-to-make torte from the capital city of Budapest is a lovely combination of hazelnut, walnut, chocolate, and orange flavors. Serve it with afternoon coffee on a chilly day.

Cake layers

6 large eggs, at room temperature
¾ cup granulated sugar
Vanilla extract
1¼ cups hazelnut flour (made from about 5 ounces or 1⅛ cups toasted, skinned hazelnuts)
1¼ cups walnut flour (made from about 4½ ounces or 1¼ cups walnut halves)
1 teaspoon baking powder
Finely grated zest of 1 orange
3 ounces semi-sweet chocolate, grated

Garnish

2 cups heavy whipping cream, very cold
¼ cup confectioners' sugar
2 ounces grated or shaved semi-sweet chocolate

▶ Preheat the oven to 325°F. Line the bottom of a 9-inch-diameter round springform pan with parchment paper. Butter the paper and sides of the pan. Sprinkle with flour, shaking off the excess.

▶ **Cake layers:** In the bowl of a stand mixer fitted with the whisk attachment, beat the eggs and sugar on high speed for about 10 minutes until light and fluffy. The mixture will resemble whipped cream. Add the vanilla and mix until combined.

● In a medium bowl, whisk together the hazelnut and walnut flours, baking powder, orange zest, and grated chocolate. Gradually fold these dry ingredients into the egg mixture until well combined.

- Pour into the prepared pan, smoothing the top with a spatula. Bake on the middle rack of the oven at 325°F for 30 to 40 minutes, until the top feels firm to the touch and a toothpick inserted in the center comes out clean. Let the cake cool in the pan set on a wire rack for at least 1 hour. (**Note:** You can make this torte a day in advance, wrap in plastic, refrigerate it overnight, and garnish with whipped cream before serving.)

▶ **Garnish:** Chill a mixing bowl and mixer whisk attachment in the freezer. Whip the cream to soft peaks in the chilled bowl, gradually adding the confectioners' sugar. Beat until stiff peaks form.

▶ **Assembly:** Remove the cake from the pan and slice it horizontally into two layers. Spread some whipped cream on the bottom layer, then put the other layer on top. Cover the top and sides with whipped cream, saving any extra to serve with each slice. Sprinkle the grated or shaved chocolate over the top of the torte.

▶ Makes 8 to 10 servings.

Chocolate-Raspberry Torte

The combination of raspberries and chocolate is a marriage made in heaven. Making this pretty four-layer torte is a real production, but once you've tasted it, you'll know why it's worth the effort.

First cake layers

4 large eggs, at room temperature
3 tablespoons granulated sugar
1 cup walnut flour (made from about 3½ ounces or 1 cup walnut halves)
2 ounces semi-sweet chocolate, coarsely grated

Second cake layers

4 large eggs, at room temperature
3 tablespoons granulated sugar
1¼ cups almond flour (made from about 5 ounces or 1 cup of unblanched almonds)

Filling

1 cup milk
3 large egg yolks
3 tablespoons all-purpose flour
¼ cup confectioners' sugar

First filling addition

3 ounces semi-sweet chocolate, grated

Second filling addition

2 tablespoons seedless raspberry jam
2 tablespoons rum
1 tablespoon raspberry syrup

Raspberry glaze

12 ounces raspberry preserves
2 tablespoons water

Chocolate glaze

¼ cup warm water
4 ounces semi-sweet chocolate, grated
4 teaspoons unsalted butter, at room temperature

Garnish

1 cup heavy whipping cream, very cold
2 tablespoons confectioners' sugar
Fresh raspberries

► Preheat the oven to 325°F. Line the bottom of two 9-inch-diameter round springform pans with parchment paper. Butter the paper and sides of the pans. Sprinkle with flour, shaking off the excess.

► **First cake layers:** In the bowl of a stand mixer fitted with the whisk attachment, beat the eggs and sugar at high speed for about 10 minutes, until light and fluffy. The mixture will resemble whipped cream.

  • Combine the walnut flour and grated chocolate in a separate small bowl. Gradually fold this mixture into the egg-sugar mixture until well combined. Pour the batter into one of the prepared pans, smoothing the top with a spatula. Cover and refrigerate it until the second layer is ready.

► **Second cake layers:** In the bowl of a stand mixer fitted with the whisk attachment beat the eggs and the sugar on high speed for about 10 minutes, until light and fluffy. The mixture will resemble whipped cream. Gradually fold the almond flour into the egg-sugar mixture. Pour the batter into the second prepared pan, smoothing the top with a spatula.

  • Place both pans of batter on the middle rack of the oven and bake at 325°F for 25 minutes or until the top feels firm to the touch and a toothpick inserted into the center comes out clean.

(**Note:** If you can't fit both pans in the oven at the same time, bake the first cake and refrigerate the pan with the batter for the second cake while the first one is baking. Then bake the second cake.) Let the cakes cool in the pans set on a wire rack.

▶ **Filling:** Warm the milk to lukewarm in the top of a metal double boiler set over, but not touching, simmering water. Remove the pan from the heat. Pour ½ cup of the warm milk into a small bowl. Whisk the egg yolks and flour into this milk. Strain through a sieve into the remaining milk in the top of the double boiler. Place the pan back on the heat and stir the mixture until it thickens. Take the pan off the heat and remove the top of the double boiler, setting it in a pan with 2 inches of ice water to stop the cooking. Stir in the confectioners' sugar.

- Divide this filling mixture in half. Add the grated chocolate to one half, stirring to mix well.

- Stir together the raspberry jam, rum, and raspberry syrup in a small bowl. Add this to the other half of the filling mixture, stirring to mix well.

▶ **Assembly:** Carefully cut each cake in half horizontally. Remove the parchment paper. Place one chocolate-walnut layer on a cake plate and cover the top with half of the chocolate filling. Place an almond cake layer on top of that and cover with all of the raspberry cream. Put the remaining chocolate-walnut cake layer on top of the raspberry cream, and top the cake with the remaining chocolate filling. Finally, place the remaining almond cake layer on top.

▶ **Raspberry glaze:** Combine the raspberry preserves and water in a small saucepan. Slowly bring to a boil over medium heat, stirring often. The mixture will be very thick. Strain through a sieve. Measure out ¼ cup and save the remaining glaze for another torte.

- Spread ¼ cup of the warm glaze on top of the almond cake layer. Put the torte in the refrigerator and chill until the glaze sets and you are ready to cover with the chocolate glaze.

▶ **Chocolate glaze:** Put ¼ cup of warm water and the grated chocolate into the top of a double boiler set over, but not touching, simmering water. Stir until chocolate is nearly melted, then remove from the heat. Remove the top pan and let it sit until the chocolate is completely melted. Then stir in the room-temperature butter cut into small pieces. Stir until well combined. The mixture will be thin but will thicken as it cools.

- When the chocolate glaze has cooled slightly, pour it all onto the center of the torte. Using a spatula, quickly smooth the glaze over the top and sides of the torte. Refrigerate.

▶ **Garnish:** Chill a mixing bowl and mixer whisk attachment in the freezer. Whip the cream to soft peaks, gradually adding confectioners' sugar. Beat until stiff peaks form.

- Put whipped cream in a pastry bag fitted with a large star-tip nozzle. Pipe rosettes of whipped cream around the outside edge of the top of the torte and top each rosette with a fresh raspberry. Serve extra whipped cream and raspberries, if desired, with each slice.

▶ Makes 16 very rich servings.

HUNGARIAN RASPBERRIES

Hungarians love raspberries. Some Hungarians still enjoy the old-fashioned pleasure of searching for wild raspberries in the forests in the summer. Others grow raspberry bushes in their home gardens or buy boxes of the fragile red berries at the farmers' markets.

They eat raspberries fresh, cook them into compotes and puddings, puree them into cold soups, preserve them as jams, use them in baking, and freeze them into ice cream and sorbets. They macerate raspberries in rum, ferment them into wine, turn them into sweet liqueurs, and distill them into clear brandies. And before the advent of commercial soft drinks, Hungarians used to boil raspberry juice and sugar into a sweet syrup, cool and bottle it, then combine it with bubbly Seltzer water in a 3-to-1 ratio to make a refreshing nonalcoholic drink.

During the last four decades of the twentieth century, Hungary was one of the world's largest exporters of raspberries, with many thousands of acres planted with raspberry bushes. But during the past twenty years, raspberry production in Hungary has dropped precipitously because of climate change (hotter temperatures, less rain), plant diseases, labor shortages and higher costs, and competition from other European countries, especially Poland, which is now the largest grower of raspberries in the European Union. From once being a major producer and exporter of the tasty red berries, Hungary now has to import them to meet consumer demand.[15]

Editor

Malakoff Cream Torte

This is one version of the classic cream torte named for the Battle of Malakoff in the Crimean War. Made of sponge cake laced with rum, my recipe uses ground walnuts in the cake batter and ground almonds in the buttercream, with whipped cream for decorating the top of the torte.

Cake layers

6 large eggs, at room temperature
5 tablespoons granulated sugar
1 cup plus 2 tablespoons all-purpose flour
½ cup plus 1 tablespoon walnut flour (made from 2 ounces or ½ cup of walnut halves)
½ teaspoon baking powder

Filling

1 cup confectioners' sugar
½ stick (4 tablespoons, 2 ounces, ¼ cup) unsalted butter, at room temperature
1 cup almond flour (made from 3½ ounces or ⅔ cup unblanched almonds)
½ cup milk

Assembly

½ cup dark rum (to moisten the cake layers)

Garnish

1 cup heavy whipping cream, very cold
2 tablespoons granulated sugar

▶ Preheat the oven to 325°F. Line the bottom of a 10-inch-diameter round springform pan with parchment paper. Butter the paper and the sides of the pan. Sprinkle with flour, shaking out the excess flour.

► **Cake layers:** In the bowl of a stand mixer fitted with the whisk attachment, beat the eggs with the sugar at high speed for about 10 minutes, or until the eggs resemble whipped cream.

- In a separate bowl, whisk together the all-purpose flour, walnut flour, and baking powder. Fold this flour mixture into the egg-sugar mixture. Pour the batter into the prepared pan, smoothing out the top with a spatula.

- Bake at 325°F for 25 to 30 minutes, or until the top feels firm to the touch. Let the cake cool in the pan set on a wire rack.

► **Filling:** Using a handheld mixer, beat the butter with the sugar in a medium-size bowl until light and fluffy, about 5 minutes. In another bowl stir together the almond flour and milk, then add to the butter mixture. Beat until all ingredients are well incorporated (about 2 minutes).

► **Assembly:** Remove the cake from the pan and cut it horizontally into three layers. Sprinkle the bottom layer with 4 tablespoons of the rum. Spread one-fourth of the almond-buttercream filling evenly on top. Add the next cake layer, sprinkle with the remaining rum, and spread one-fourth of the filling evenly on top. Add the top cake layer, then cover the top and all sides with the remaining almond buttercream. Refrigerate for at least 3 hours or overnight. (**Note:** You can also freeze the torte for three months, wrapped securely in plastic wrap.)

► **Garnish:** Chill a mixing bowl and mixer whisk attachment in the freezer. Whip the cream to soft peaks in the chilled bowl, gradually adding the sugar. Beat until stiff peaks form.

- Bring the cake to room temperature. Decorate it with whipped cream, piping rosettes on the top with a pastry bag fitted with a star tip.

► Makes 8 to 10 servings.

Malakow-Torte

Zutaten sind: 40 Stück Biskotten, 6 d. Zucker,
Saft ½ Orange, Rum, 15 d. Butter, 10 d. Zucker
2 Dotter 10 d. Mandeln oder Haselnüsse ¼ l. Schlag-
obers zum überziehen u. spritzen.
Einen geölten Tortenreifen setzt man auf eine
Glas oder Porzellanplatte u. belegt den Boden
mit Biskotten. Zucker (6 d.) spinnt man mit
wenig Wasser, mengt den Orangensaft Rum u.
tropft diese Mischung auf die Biskotten. Dann
bestreicht man sie mit der Crème, stellt am
Rand halbe in die Zuckerlösung getauchte Biskotten. Nun macht man eine zweite Reihe von
den vorhandenen Biskotten u crème. Am näch-
sten Tag übersieht u. spritzt man sie mit Schlago-
bers. Crème: Butter, Zucker, Dotter abtreiben
aus den Mandeln oder Haselnüsse Grillage wo-

Malakoff Torte II   Frau Halla

8 d. Butter abtreiben mit 10 d. Zucker, 2 Dotter u.
10 d. geschälte geriebene Mandeln u. ¼ l. Milch,
eine Stunde lang! Mit Biskotten reihenweise
eine Tortenform auslegen, dazwischen den Abtrieb
geben. 24 Stunden stehen lassen mit Oberschaum
verzieren. (Den Tortenreif ohne Boden auf eine Glasplatte stellen, welchen man vorsichtig
entfernen kann.)

Two different recipes for Malakoff Torte, handwritten (in German),
from Belli Tante's personal collection of recipes.

MALAKOFF TORTE

Malakoff (or Malakov) Torte is often cited as an example of a torte named for a place or an event, instead of a particular person or just the main ingredient of the torte. In this case it was the decisive Battle of Malakoff during the Crimean War, which was fought between the French and Russian armies in September 1855, during the Siege of Sevastopol. The name refers to Malakoff Ridge on one of the fortified hills surrounding the Bay of Sevastopol, which was stormed by French troops and successfully taken, thus ending the thirteen-month siege.[16]

But why a cream cake? Albert Shumate, a California historian, claims that in celebration of the victory a cake of enormous dimensions, representing Fort Malakoff, was baked in San Francisco the following November.[17] On the other hand, the noted Hungarian chef George Lang, in his classic cookbook, *The Cuisine of Hungary*, gives "a friend's family recipe [for Malakoff Torte] at least three generations old" and states, "Like Nesselrode [Pudding], named for another Russian general-aristocrat, Malakoff originated in the Russian kitchen. It was probably brought back by French chefs and then copied by other European chefs. There are at least half a dozen recipes for cooked Malakoff cream, and another half dozen for cold preparations."[18] So does Malakoff not refer to the battle at all?

Whatever its origin, Malakoff Torte is traditionally a layered cream torte, with many variations. The layers can be ladyfingers (homemade or store-bought), sponge cake rounds, or even sometimes nut meringues (*dacquoises*) or choux pastry, dipped in or sprinkled with rum, maraschino, or other liquor. The filling is a custard cream, buttercream, or gelatin-stabilized Bavarian cream, often flavored with more liquor or perhaps even with coffee or fruit. The torte is then frosted with whipped cream and sometimes decorated with toasted almonds or maraschino cherries. Some bakers insist that a Malakoff Torte should never contain chocolate, but that rule was meant to be broken by cooks who couldn't resist adding another ingredient to the mix. There are even tortes called Malakoff made entirely of chocolate sponge cake and chocolate custard cream.[19]

And when you think of it, a torte made by dipping ladyfingers in sweet liquor, layering them with a rich cream filling, maybe sprinkling chocolate over the top, and adding whipped cream, too, sounds suspiciously like a kissing cousin of Italian tiramisu, not to mention Italian zuppa inglese and British trifle. Regardless of its origin, Malakoff Torte became a beloved member of the Austro-Hungarian pastry shop repertoire in the second half of the nineteenth century and remains so today.

Editor

Date-Nut Torte

One snowy afternoon in Connecticut, when we were visiting Belli Tante—the dear Hungarian woman who introduced me to her own homemade nut-flour tortes—she served us this delicious date torte, which is typical of those that were offered at tearooms and coffeehouses in Vienna and Budapest. Enjoy it with your favorite hot brew.

Cake layers

10 large egg whites, at room temperature
Pinch of salt
6 tablespoons granulated sugar
3½ cups almond flour (made from about 12 ounces or 2¼ cups blanched almonds)
3½ cups toasted hazelnut flour (made from about 13 ounces or 2⅝ cups of toasted, skinned hazelnuts)
3½ ounces semi-sweet chocolate, grated
9 ounces large pitted dates, thinly sliced lengthwise

Filling

2 sticks (16 tablespoons, 8 ounces, 1 cup) unsalted butter, at room temperature
1 cup confectioners' sugar
4 egg yolks, lightly beaten with a fork
¼ cup very strong espresso coffee (decaffeinated can be used)
1 vanilla bean, cut in half lengthwise (or 1 teaspoon vanilla extract)
6 tablespoons granulated sugar
6 tablespoons cocoa powder (not Dutch process)

Garnish

2 cups heavy whipping cream, very cold
¼ cup confectioners' sugar

▶ Preheat the oven to 325°F. Line the bottom of an 11 × 17–inch rimmed baking sheet with parchment paper. Butter the paper and sides of pan. Sprinkle with flour, shaking off the excess.

▶ **Cake layers:** In the bowl of a stand mixer fitted with the whisk attachment, beat the egg whites with a pinch of salt until soft peaks form. Continue to beat, gradually adding the sugar until stiff peaks form that are still glossy, not dry.

- In another large bowl, whisk together the almond and hazelnut flours, then add the grated chocolate. Gradually and gently fold this mixture into the beaten egg whites until thoroughly combined.

- Pour three-fourths of the batter into the prepared pan, spreading it evenly. Place all but one ounce of the date slices in even rows across the top of the batter. (Set the remaining date slices aside.) Spread the remaining one-fourth of the batter evenly over the dates in the pan.

- Bake on the middle rack of the oven at 325°F for 20 minutes, or until the top feels firm to the touch. Turn off the oven, leave the oven door closed, and let the cake layer stay inside the oven for 10 more minutes. Then let the cake cool in the pan set on a wire rack for at least 1 hour.

▶ **Filling:** Put the egg yolks, espresso coffee, and vanilla bean in the top of a metal double boiler set over, but not touching, simmering water. Stir constantly until the mixture starts to thicken. Take the pan off the heat, remove the top of the double boiler, and set it in a larger bowl with 2 inches of ice water to stop the cooking. Keep stirring the mixture until it has cooled. Remove the vanilla bean and scrape the seeds into the custard. (Or, if substituting vanilla extract, stir it into the custard mixture.) Whisk together the sugar and cocoa powder in another bowl, then whisk this mixture into the custard.

- Using an electric mixer on medium speed, beat the butter and sugar in a medium bowl until light and fluffy. Gradually add the custard mixture, slowly beating together until well incorporated.

▶ **Assembly:** Based on your serving platter size, select the size of torte that best fits your needs.

Option 1: Cut the cake layer into three long strips, each 17 inches long and about 3½ inches wide.

Option 2: Cut the cake layer into three long strips, each 11 inches long and 5½ inches wide.

- Place one cake layer on a long serving platter. Spread one-third of the filling on that bottom cake layer, then put another cake layer on top of it and spread with one-third of the filling. Place the last cake layer on top. Trim the short ends to even out the edges and the long sides if necessary. Then cover only the top with the remaining filling.

▶ **Garnish:** Chill a mixing bowl and a mixer whisk attachment in the freezer. Whip the cream in the chilled bowl to soft peaks, gradually adding the confectioners' sugar. Beat until stiff peaks form.

- Spread the whipped cream on the sides of the torte, then use a cake comb to make wavy lines on the whipped cream. If desired, pipe a border of whipped cream around the top and bottom edges using a star-tip nozzle on a pastry bag. Line the remaining date slices down the center of the torte.

- Refrigerate the torte for a few hours, taking it out of the refrigerator about 30 minutes before serving. (**Note:** You can make this torte a day in advance, refrigerate it overnight, and garnish with whipped cream just before serving.)

▶ Makes 10 to 16 servings, depending on length of torte.

TEA WITH TORTES

When Belli Tante served us her Date Torte on that snowy winter day, to help us warm up she poured one of her unusual specialty teas. When we asked, "Where did she get this wonderful tea?" she told us the story of a woman named Mizzi who was known throughout Vienna for her variety of teas. Mizzi's career began on the eve of World War II. A Jewish couple who sold teas was hurriedly preparing to flee Austria as the Nazis advanced, and they asked Mizzi to take care of their shop during their absence. Sadly, they never returned. But Mizzi made their little shop, located next to the Opera House, into an elegant culinary landmark. Soon no well-to-do family in Vienna would be without her teas, especially her famous Diplomaten tea. Each customer would pick out a particular blend, then Mizzi would retire behind a heavy curtain, where she blended the final mixture in secret. Unfortunately, Mizzi's teas were no longer available by the time we knew Belli Tante, so we were treated to another of her favorite specialty teas that day.

Ella Szabó

Walnut Wedding Torte with Hazelnut Filling

One day in 1980, a young bride-to-be surprised me with a telephone call. She had attended a friend's wedding in Chicago, where she had tasted a torte made from toasted hazelnut flour baked by the famous Hungarian chef Louis Szathmáry, who was now living in the United States. When she returned home to Connecticut, she very much wanted to serve a similar torte at her own wedding. Would I make it for her? Could I do it? I couldn't resist the challenge, so I created this torte, which soon became my most requested torte for weddings. Guests always asked for second helpings! Our daughter, Eve, chose it for her wedding cake as well. It's ideal for other special occasions and large parties—any time you're entertaining a crowd.

▶ **NOTE:** You can make this torte a day in advance, refrigerate it over-night, and garnish it with the buttercream just before serving. Or you can wrap the frosted torte (without the meringue buttercream decorations) tightly in plastic wrap and freeze it for up to two months. Decorate with buttercream before serving.

Cake layers

10 large eggs, at room temperature
9 tablespoons of granulated sugar
2½ cups walnut flour (made from about 9 ounces or 2½ cups walnut halves)

Hazelnut filling

1 large egg, at room temperature
1 tablespoon all-purpose flour
1 cup whole milk, at room temperature
1 tablespoon pure vanilla extract
2 cups hazelnut flour (made from about 8 ounces or 1½ cups toasted, skinned hazelnuts)

A slice of Walnut Wedding Torte with Hazelnut Filling.

2 sticks (16 tablespoons, 8 ounces, 1 cup) unsalted butter, at
 room temperature
½ cup granulated sugar

Meringue buttercream

2 cups granulated sugar
½ cup water
1 cup egg whites (about 8 large whites)
Pinch of cream of tartar
6 sticks (48 tablespoons, 24 ounces, 3 cups) unsalted butter, at
 room temperature

▶ Preheat the oven to 325°F. Line the bottom of an 11 × 17–inch rimmed
 baking sheet with parchment paper. Butter the paper and sides of the pan.
 Sprinkle with flour, shaking off the excess.

▶ **Cake layers:** In a *6-quart bowl* of a stand mixer fitted with the whisk
 attachment, beat the eggs and sugar at high speed for about 10 minutes
 until light and fluffy, resembling whipped cream. Gradually fold in the
 walnut flour, blending thoroughly.

   • Spread the batter evenly on the prepared baking pan, smoothing the
    top with a spatula. Bake on the middle rack of the oven at 325°F for
    about 15 minutes, or until the top feels firm to the touch. Let the
    cake cool in the pan set on a wire rack.

▶ **Hazelnut filling:** Lightly whisk the egg in a medium bowl. Add the flour,
 milk, and vanilla, whisking to dissolve the flour. Strain this mixture into
 the top of a metal double boiler set over, but not touching, simmering
 water. Cook, stirring constantly, for about 5 minutes or until the mixture
 thickens. Remove the pan from the heat and set the top pan in a bowl
 of ice water to stop the cooking. Stir until lukewarm, then fold in the
 hazelnut flour. Let cool to room temperature.

   • In the bowl of a stand mixer fitted with the paddle attachment, beat
    the butter and sugar on high speed for about 4 minutes or until
    light and fluffy. Gradually add the cooled hazelnut custard to the
    butter-sugar mixture, mixing on low speed until well incorporated.
    (The two mixtures should be the same temperature to ensure an

even mix.) Cover and refrigerate for 30 minutes or until the filling is firm enough to spread.

▶ **Meringue buttercream:** Combine the sugar and the water in a heavy saucepan. Bring to a boil over high heat, then boil, without stirring, until a candy thermometer reads 238°F.

- In the bowl of a stand mixer fitted with the whisk attachment, beat the egg whites and cream of tartar together on high speed until very stiff peaks form that are still glossy, not dry. With the mixer running on low, slowly dribble the hot sugar syrup into the egg whites. Increase mixer speed to high and continue to beat until the meringue is no longer hot. Set aside.

- In another bowl of the stand mixer, now fitted with the paddle attachment, beat the butter until light and fluffy. Slowly add the slightly warm meringue to the butter, beating until the mixture is smooth.

▶ **Assembly:** Based on your serving platter size, select the size of torte that best fits your needs.

Option 1: Cut the cake layer into three long strips, each 17 inches long and about 3½ inches wide.

Option 2: Cut the cake layer into three long strips, each 11 inches long and 5½ inches wide.

- Place one strip of cake on a long serving platter. Spread one-half of the hazelnut filling evenly on that cake layer, then add the next cake layer. Spread the remaining one-half of the filling on it and top with the last cake layer. Trim the short ends to even out the edges and the long sides if necessary.

- Cover the top and sides of the torte evenly with the buttercream. Spoon any remaining buttercream into a pastry bag and pipe decorations as desired on the torte.

- Refrigerate for at least 2 hours or overnight. To serve, cut slices slightly less than 1 inch thick.

▶ Makes 10 to 16 servings, depending on length of torte.

Macadamia Nut Torte

My immediate family now lives in the San Francisco area of California, and they frequently fly to their favorite vacation place, Hawaii. Returning from one of their trips, they surprised me with a box full of heavenly rich macadamia nuts. Eve, my daughter, said to me, "Why don't you try to create a one-of-a-kind macadamia nut torte?" So I worked at testing and retesting this recipe until I came up with this delicious torte that makes the most of that luscious Hawaiian gift.

Caramelized macadamia-nut flour

½ pound (8 ounces) whole macadamia nuts
1 cup granulated sugar

Cake layers

9 large eggs, at room temperature
½ cup granulated sugar
2 cups walnut flour (made from about 7 ounces or 2 cups walnut halves)

Filling

½ cup milk, plus 1 tablespoon milk (divided use)
2 large egg yolks
4 teaspoons all-purpose flour
1½ cups caramelized macadamia-nut flour (from recipe above)
2 sticks (16 tablespoons, 8 ounces, 1 cup) unsalted butter, at room temperature
2 tablespoons granulated sugar

Garnish

1 cup heavy whipping cream, very cold
2 tablespoons confectioners' sugar

► **Caramelized macadamia-nut flour:** Set the oven at 225°F. Set aside 5 to 7 macadamia nuts for the garnish. Place remaining nuts in a shallow baking pan and place the pan on a rack in the middle of the oven. Toast the nuts for 10 minutes. Then increase the oven temperature to 300°F and bake for another 10 minutes, shaking the pan frequently. Nuts should be a light toasty brown in color. Remove from the oven and let cool completely.

- Heavily butter or oil a nonstick rimmed baking sheet. Heat the sugar in a medium saucepan over low heat, stirring constantly to melt the sugar and cooking until it is liquid and dark in color. Pour the whole macadamia nuts into the pan and stir them immediately. Quickly remove the pan from the heat and pour the nut mixture onto the prepared baking sheet. Let it cool for at least 30 minutes. Do not touch with your fingers because it will burn you. After the mixture has completely cooled, break it up into pieces. Grind these clumps in a nut grinder or food processor to make the caramelized nut flour. Measure out 1½ cups and set aside.

▶ **Cake layers:** Preheat the oven to 325°F. Line an 11 × 17–inch rimmed baking sheet with parchment paper. Butter the paper and sides of the pan. Sprinkle with flour, shaking off the excess.

- In a *6-quart bowl* of a stand mixer fitted with the whisk attachment, beat the eggs and the sugar at high speed for 10 to 15 minutes, until light and fluffy. The mixture will resemble whipped cream.
- Gradually fold in the walnut flour. Pour the batter into the prepared pan and smooth the top with a spatula.
- Bake on the middle rack of the oven at 325°F for 15 to 20 minutes, until the top feels firm to the touch. Let the cake cool in the pan set on a wire rack.

▶ **Filling:** Put ½ cup of milk into the top of a metal double boiler set over, but not touching, simmering water. Heat the milk to lukewarm. In another bowl beat the egg yolks lightly with the remaining 1 tablespoon of milk and the flour, mixing to a smooth consistency.

- Pour the egg-flour mixture through a sieve into the milk in the double boiler. Whisk constantly over moderate heat until the mixture looks thick like a pudding. Take the pan off the heat, remove the top of the double boiler, and set it in a bowl with 2 inches of ice water to stop the cooking. Stir until lukewarm. Stir in the caramelized nut flour.

- In the bowl of a stand mixer fitted with the paddle attachment, beat the butter with the sugar until light and fluffy. With the mixer on low speed, gradually add the egg-nut-flour mixture until well incorporated. Cover and refrigerate for 1 hour or until well chilled before using.

▶ **Garnish:** Chill a mixing bowl and mixer whisk attachment in the freezer. Whip the cream to soft peaks in the chilled bowl, gradually adding the confectioners' sugar. Beat until stiff peaks form.

▶ **Assembly:** Based on your serving platter size, select the size of torte that best fits your needs.

Option 1: Cut the cake layer into three long strips, each 17 inches long and about 3½ inches wide.

Option 2: Cut the cake layer into three long strips, each 11 inches long and 5½ inches wide.

- Place one strip on a long serving platter. Spread one-fourth of the filling evenly on that bottom cake layer. Add the next cake layer and spread with one-fourth of the filling. Place the third cake layer on top. Trim the short ends to even out the edges and the long sides if necessary. Cover only the sides with the remaining filling.

- Fill a star-tipped pastry bag with the whipped cream and make small rosettes very close to each other to cover the entire top of the torte. Decorate the top with 5 to 7 whole toasted macadamia nuts placed in a row in the center. Refrigerate for at least 1 hour. To serve, cut crosswise into 1-inch-thick pieces.

▶ Makes 10 to 16 servings, depending on length of torte.

NUT-FLOUR ROULADES

▶ **NOTE:** In these recipes, volume measurements of *nut flours* (in cups) are an approximation, to the nearest fraction of a cup, based on grinding the amount of *whole nuts* listed in the recipe. Volume measurements of nut flours can vary slightly, depending on the size of the nuts and the method used for grinding them. Since hand-ground nut flours are fluffier and less dense than store-bought nut flours, the volume of hand-ground nut flour can be slightly larger than the volume of store-bought nut flour, even though they both weigh the same. Likewise, tortes made with commercially ground nut flours tend to be a bit denser than those made with nuts ground by hand.

For best results measure out the amount of *whole nuts* needed in a recipe (in cups, or by weight in ounces), then grind them in your own kitchen and use the amount of nut flour that you produce. If using *store-bought nut flour*, then use the number of cups of *nut flour* specified in the recipe.

Hazelnut Roulade with Buttercream Filling

Using the correct pan size is very important in this recipe. Both the roulade and the garnish can be made in advance and refrigerated until needed.

Cake

6 large eggs, separated, at room temperature
Pinch of salt
½ cup granulated sugar
5 tablespoons toasted hazelnut flour (made from 1½ ounces or ⅓ cup whole, skinned hazelnuts)
2 tablespoons all-purpose flour

Filling

3 ounces semi-sweet chocolate
1 tablespoon water
1 stick (8 tablespoons, 4 ounces, ½ cup) unsalted butter, at room temperature, cut into small pieces
3 tablespoons confectioners' sugar
¾ cup coarsely chopped toasted hazelnuts

Garnish

1 cup heavy whipping cream, very cold
2 tablespoons confectioners' sugar
Toasted whole hazelnuts

▶ Preheat the oven to 300°F. Line the bottom of a 10 × 15–inch jelly-roll pan with parchment paper. Butter the paper and sides of the pan. Sprinkle with flour, shaking off the excess.

▶ **Cake:** In the bowl of a stand mixer fitted with the whisk attachment, beat the egg whites with a pinch of salt until stiff peaks form that are still glossy, not dry. Set aside.

- In another bowl of the stand mixer fitted with the paddle attachment, beat the egg yolks with the sugar for 5 minutes on high speed, until light colored and a ribbon forms when the paddle is lifted. Gradually fold the egg whites into this egg mixture.
- In a separate bowl, whisk the hazelnut flour and all-purpose flour together, then fold this flour mixture into the egg mixture until well combined.
- Spread the batter evenly in the prepared pan, smoothing over the top. Bake on the middle rack of the oven at 300°F for 12 to 15 minutes. When the cake is firm to the touch, turn off the heat, keep the oven door closed, and leave the pan in the oven for 2 more minutes. Let the cake cool in the pan set on a wire rack.

▶ **Filling:** Fill the bottom pan of a double boiler with only enough water to keep from touching the bottom of the top pan. Place the chocolate and 1 tablespoon of water in the top pan and set aside. Bring the water in the double boiler to a boil, then turn off the heat and place the pan containing the chocolate over the hot water. Stir until the chocolate is melted, then remove the top pan and set aside, letting the chocolate cool to room temperature. Add the butter and the sugar to the chocolate, stirring gently to combine well. Then gently stir in the toasted hazelnuts, mixing well. Refrigerate for 20 minutes before using.

▶ **Assembly:** Spread the buttercream filling evenly on the cake layer, still in the baking pan. Starting with the long side, carefully roll it up into a roulade, peeling off the parchment paper as you roll. Refrigerate for 2 hours. Before serving, you might want to decorate the top with whole toasted hazelnuts and serve with a dollop of whipped cream.

▶ **Garnish:** Chill a mixing bowl and mixer whisk attachment in the freezer. Whip the cream to soft peaks in the chilled bowl, gradually adding the confectioners' sugar. Beat until stiff peaks form. Refrigerate until needed.

- To serve, slice crosswise with a serrated knife into rounds approximately 1 inch thick. Garnish with sweetened whipped cream and a few toasted whole hazelnuts, if desired.

▶ Makes 14 to 16 servings.

Hungarian Hazelnut Roulade with Buttercream Filling.

ROULADES

Roulade is the French word for something that is rolled up. In culinary terms a rolled-up food can be savory (such as a flattened piece of meat rolled around a filling) or sweet (such as a flat cake rolled up around a sweet filling). Many European languages use the term *roulade* (or some version of it) to refer to rolled-up foods.

Roulades often refer to cylindrical cakes made by baking a sponge cake batter or other flexible cake batter in a sheet pan, then rolling the cake up around a filling of custard cream, buttercream, stabilized whipped cream, or sometimes simply thick jam or sweetened chestnut puree. Popular cream-filling flavors are vanilla, chocolate, and coffee—and whole cherries or berries might be included in the cream filling, too. Some roulades are frosted with buttercream or whipped cream; others are simply dusted with confectioners' sugar.

These cylindrical cakes are popular in many countries, including Central Europe. In the United States, they're often called jelly rolls; in Britain they're known as Swiss rolls. The Spanish have their *brazo de gitano* (gypsy's arm), and the French love their *bûche de Noël* (Yule log) at Christmas.

Editor

Chocolate Roulade with Hazelnut Cream

This roulade has been a favorite dessert of my family and my friends for many years. Combining the cocoa-flavored sponge cake with the toasted hazelnut cream filling produces a symphony of flavors, and a little whipped cream enhances the taste even more.

Cake

6 large eggs, at room temperature
½ cup granulated sugar
3 tablespoons cocoa powder (not Dutch process)
⅓ cup all-purpose flour

Filling

½ cup whole milk, at room temperature
2 cups toasted hazelnut flour (made from about 7½ ounces or 1½ cups toasted whole hazelnuts)
1¼ sticks (10 tablespoons, 5 ounces) unsalted butter, at room temperature
5 tablespoons granulated sugar

Garnish (optional)

1 cup heavy whipping cream, very cold
2 tablespoons confectioners' sugar
10 whole toasted hazelnuts

▶ Preheat the oven to 300°F. Line the bottom of a 10 × 15–inch jelly-roll pan with parchment paper. Butter the parchment and sides of pan. Sprinkle with flour, shaking off the excess.

▶ Cake: Using a stand mixer fitted with the whisk attachment, beat the eggs with the sugar at high speed until light and fluffy, about 10 minutes or until the mixture resembles whipped cream.

● Whisk the cocoa powder and flour together in a bowl, then fold into the egg mixture until well combined. Do not overmix; it is better to have a somewhat lumpy batter. Spread the batter evenly in the prepared pan. Bake for about 12 to 15 minutes, until the top springs back when gently pressed. Turn off the oven, keep the oven door closed, and leave the pan in the oven for 2 to 3 minutes more. Then let the cake cool completely in the pan set on a wire rack.

▶ **Filling:** Bring the milk to a boil in a small saucepan. Pour the hot milk into a medium heatproof bowl and stir in the hazelnut flour. Let cool completely.

- Using a handheld mixer, beat the butter with the sugar in a medium-large bowl until the sugar is fully incorporated and the butter is smooth. Add the hazelnut-milk mixture and beat together at low speed for 1 minute more. Cover and refrigerate for 1 hour.

▶ **Assembly:** Spread the filling evenly on the cake layer. Starting with the long side of the cake, roll it up, peeling off the parchment paper as you roll. Refrigerate for 2 hours or freeze for up to three months in a ziplock freezer bag. Thaw for 2 hours at room temperature before serving.

▶ **Garnish:** Chill a mixing bowl and mixer whisk attachment in the freezer. Whip the cream to soft peaks in the chilled bowl, gradually adding the sugar. Beat until stiff peaks form.

- To serve the roulade, slice crosswise with a serrated knife into rounds, approximately 1½ inches thick. Garnish with sweetened whipped cream and a few toasted whole hazelnuts, if desired.

▶ Makes 10 servings.

Walnut Roulade with Walnut Buttercream Filling

Since nuts ripen in the fall, this roulade is perfect for an autumn or winter treat.

Cake

5 large eggs
Pinch of salt
5 tablespoons granulated sugar
5 tablespoons walnut flour (made from 1 ounce or ⅓ cup walnut halves)
2 tablespoons all-purpose flour

Filling

1 cup walnut flour (made from 3 ounces or 1 cup walnuts)
¾ cup confectioners' sugar
½ cup milk
1 tablespoon cornstarch
1 large egg yolk
1½ sticks (12 tablespoons, 6 ounces, ¾ cup) unsalted butter, at room temperature, cut into tablespoons
1 tablespoon dark rum
6 toasted walnut halves

Garnish

1 cup heavy whipping cream, very cold
1 tablespoon confectioners' sugar

Hungarian Walnut Roulade with Walnut Buttercream Filling.

▶ Preheat the oven to 300°F. Line a 10 × 15–inch jelly-roll pan with parchment paper. Butter the parchment paper and sides of the pan. Sprinkle with flour and shake off the excess.

▶ **Cake:** In the bowl of a stand mixer fitted with the whisk attachment, beat the eggs and sugar at high speed for about 10 minutes until light and fluffy. The mixture will resemble whipped cream.

- In a small bowl, mix the walnut flour with the all-purpose flour, then gradually fold this into the egg mixture until well combined.

- Pour the batter into the prepared pan and spread the top smooth with a spatula. Bake on the middle rack of the oven at 300°F for 12 to 15 minutes, until the top feels firm to the touch. When done, turn off the heat but keep the oven door closed, and leave the pan in the oven for 2 more minutes. Then let the cake cool in the pan set on a wire rack.

▶ **Filling:** Whisk together the walnut flour and the confectioners' sugar in a medium bowl. Set aside.

- Put the milk in the top of a metal double boiler set over, but not touching, simmering water. Sprinkle in the cornstarch and whisk to dissolve. Whisk in the egg yolk. Cook, whisking constantly, until the sauce is like a thick pudding. (The cornstarch will prevent the yolk from curdling.)

- Remove the top of the double boiler. Using a handheld mixer, beat for 2 minutes, then add the butter one tablespoon at a time. Add the rum and mix well. Set the pan in a bowl with 2 inches of ice water to cool it while stirring the mixture to keep it smooth. When cool, gradually beat in the walnut-flour mixture. Beat until all the ingredients are well incorporated and smooth. Cover and refrigerate for 1 hour.

▶ **Assembly:** Spread half of the filling evenly on the cake layer. Starting with the long side of the cake, roll the cake up into a long roulade, peeling off the parchment as you roll. Cover the top and all sides with the remaining filling. If desired, score the outside of the torte with a cake comb. Line the walnut halves in a row along the center of the roulade's top. Refrigerate for 2 hours.

► **Garnish:** Chill a mixing bowl and mixer whisk attachment in the freezer. Whip the cream to soft peaks in the chilled bowl, gradually adding the confectioners' sugar until stiff peaks form. Serve the roulade cut crosswise into approximately 1-inch-thick slices, garnished with dollops of whipped cream.

► Makes 14 to 16 servings.

Walnut Roulade with Strawberry Filling

This rich-tasting roulade can be made with either fresh strawberries in the spring or quinces that ripen in the fall. See the end of the recipe for instructions on how to make a quince filling.

Cake

8 large eggs, at room temperature
7 tablespoons of granulated sugar
2 cups walnut flour (made from about 7 ounces or 2 cups walnut halves)

Filling

2 teaspoons unflavored gelatin
8 teaspoons cold water
2 cups heavy whipping cream, very cold
½ cup confectioners' sugar
1 pound (16 ounces) strawberries, stemmed and cut into ½-inch pieces

Garnish

Confectioners' sugar
3 stemmed strawberries of similar size, for decoration

▶ Preheat the oven to 350°F. Line the bottom of an 11 × 17–inch rimmed baking sheet with parchment paper. Butter the paper and sides of the pan. Sprinkle with flour, shaking off the excess.

▶ **Cake:** In a *6-quart bowl* of a stand mixer fitted with the whisk attachment, beat the eggs and sugar at high speed for about 10 minutes, until light and fluffy. The mixture will resemble whipped cream. Gently fold in the walnut flour.

● Pour the batter into the prepared pan, smoothing over the top with a spatula. Bake at 350°F for 15 minutes. Check the top for doneness. It must feel dry. If it still feels moist, reduce the oven temperature to

250°F and bake for an additional 5 minutes. Let the cake cool in the pan set on a wire rack.

- Sprinkle a large piece of parchment paper or a clean kitchen towel with confectioners' sugar. When the cake has cooled, invert it onto the prepared surface. Pull the parchment paper from the pan off the bottom of the cake and use the sugar-dusted parchment or kitchen towel to help you roll up the pastry, to keep the cake from sticking to itself as you form it into a roll. (The parchment or towel will stay inside the roll until the cake is ready to fill.) Start rolling with one of the long edges to form a roulade (like a log), then let it cool on a rack for 30 minutes before unrolling and filling (or wrap in plastic wrap to keep for several hours, or even a day in advance, before filling and serving).

▶ **Filling:** Sprinkle the gelatin over the cold water in a small metal or heatproof glass bowl. Let it sit a few minutes to soften. Meanwhile, whip the cream in a large bowl to soft peaks, then stop beating.

- Put 1 inch of water into a small frying pan or saucepan, wider than your gelatin bowl, and bring the water to a boil. Place the gelatin bowl in the pan and turn off the heat. Leave the bowl in the pan until the gelatin is completely dissolved and looks clear. Do not stir.

- Remove the bowl from the pan and let the gelatin cool to room temperature. This happens very quickly. Beat the whipped cream again to medium peaks, then pour the dissolved room-temperature gelatin into the center at once and continue beating. Beat the confectioners' sugar into the mixture, beating only until the cream stands in stiff peaks and clings to the side of the bowl. For best decorating results, do not overwhip. The gelatin acts as a stabilizer when it is added to the whipped cream.

▶ **Assembly:** Unroll the cake layer and spread the whipped cream over the surface. Scatter the strawberry pieces over the whipped cream. Reroll the cake into a roulade, with the help of a towel or parchment paper on the outer side, if necessary. Refrigerate for 4 hours.

▶ **Garnish:** Before serving, dust the surface with confectioners' sugar and decorate the top with three whole strawberries.

▶ NOTE: This recipe also can be adapted to make a delicious Hungarian version of strawberry shortcake. Instead of rolling up the pastry, cut it into two long strips. Place one strip on the serving platter and top with the filling. Then put the second strip on top. Dust with confectioners' sugar and decorate the top with whole strawberries.

▶ Makes approximately 14 to 16 servings.

Alternative quince filling

4 large quinces, peeled and cored
1½ cups water (there should be enough water to cover the quince)
¾ cup granulated sugar
2 whole cloves

● Slice the quinces thinly, then cut each of the slices in half crosswise. Heat the water in a small pan over medium heat with the sugar and cloves until the sugar is dissolved. Add the quince and cook for 10 minutes or until the quince is soft when pierced with a fork. Remove from heat and drain the quince pieces well, also removing the cloves. Use the quince instead of the strawberry pieces in the roulade filling.

Slice of King's Torte

The King's Torte

Caramelized Hazelnut Torte with Chocolate Glaze

Chocolate-Almond Torte with Apricot Glaze

Judith's "Recovery Torte"

Belli Tante's Apple Torte

Caramelized-Almond Cream Torte

Coffee-Almond Torte

Gerbeaud Slice at Café Gerbeaud in Budapest

Classic Esterházy Torte at a coffeehouse/café in Vienna

Cherry Sponge Cake

Almond-Flour Cake with Mixed Fruits

Hungarian Cheese Biscuits (*Pogácsa*)

Vanilla Crescent Cookies

Loaves of *beigli* are a traditional treat
in Hungary at Christmas time

PART TWO

HUNGARIAN
HOMESTYLE
DESSERTS

COOKIES AND BARS

▶ **NOTE:** In these recipes, volume measurements of *nut flours* (in cups) are an approximation, to the nearest fraction of a cup, based on grinding the amount of *whole nuts* listed in the recipe. Volume measurements of nut flours can vary slightly, depending on the size of the nuts and the method used for grinding them. Since hand-ground nut flours are fluffier and less dense than store-bought nut flours, the volume of hand-ground nut flour can be slightly larger than the volume of store-bought nut flour, even though they both weigh the same. Likewise, tortes made with commercially ground nut flours tend to be a bit denser than those made with nuts ground by hand.

For best results measure out the amount of *whole nuts* needed in a recipe (in cups, or by weight in ounces), then grind them in your own kitchen and use the amount of nut flour that you produce. If using *store-bought nut flour*, then use the number of cups of *nut flour* specified in the recipe.

Vanilla Crescent Cookies

When I introduced my grandsons to cooking, this was the first recipe we made together. Their little fingers were perfect for shaping these traditional Austrian cookies. If you are looking for a fun rainy-day activity for the kids, this recipe is ideal. Imagine the children's delight when they announce to everyone at the table that they made the cookies themselves.

▶ **NOTE:** Toasting the nuts before adding them to the dough will make the flavor even richer. Toast whole nuts in a preheated 325°F oven for approximately 6 to 8 minutes. Let cool completely, then finely chop before measuring out 1½ cups of chopped nuts.

Dough

2 cups sifted all-purpose flour
2 sticks (16 tablespoons, 8 ounces, 1 cup) unsalted butter, at room temperature
½ cup confectioners' sugar
1 tablespoon pure vanilla extract
1½ cups coarsely chopped nuts (blanched almonds, macadamia nuts, hazelnuts, pecans, or walnuts)
Confectioners' sugar

Chocolate glaze

2 tablespoons (1 ounce) unsalted butter
1 tablespoon light corn syrup
5 ounces semi-sweet chocolate, grated
1 tablespoon framboise liqueur or light rum (optional)

▶ Preheat the oven to 325°F. Butter a large cookie sheet.

▶ **Dough:** Mix together the flour, butter, confectioners' sugar, and vanilla extract in a large bowl, adding the nuts last. Knead well by hand or with a stand mixer fitted with the dough hook.

● Place the dough on a lightly floured work surface. Pinch off a small piece about the size of a walnut, place it in the palm of your hand,

and roll it out into a short rope. Bend it into a crescent shape and place it on the cookie sheet. Repeat with the rest of the dough, placing the crescents 1 inch apart.

● Bake on the middle rack of the oven at 325°F for about 25 minutes. Remove the pan from the oven and lightly dust the cookies with confectioners' sugar. Let cool on the pan. Then dip the tips of the crescents into the chocolate glaze.

▶ **Chocolate glaze:** Melt the butter with the corn syrup in a small saucepan over low heat, stirring constantly. Stir in the chocolate and remove from the heat. Whisk to make a smooth glaze. Let the chocolate cool to lukewarm, then stir in the (optional) framboise or rum. Dip the tips of each crescent cookie 1 inch deep into the chocolate. Place the cookies in a row on a cookie sheet lined with wax paper or parchment paper. Refrigerate on the cookie sheet to harden the chocolate.

● Store in an airtight container, in a cool place, with each layer of cookies separated by parchment paper.

▶ Makes 28 small crescent cookies.

Vanilla Crescent Cookies are popular throughout central Europe.

VANILLA CRESCENTS

Crisp yet tender, these pale-colored, rich-tasting little cookies, traditionally made with almond flour, are popular throughout the lands of the former Austro-Hungarian Empire, as well as Germany, Switzerland, and many other Central European and Nordic countries. Occasionally they're made with toasted hazelnut flour, which produces a browner cookie. After baking, vanilla crescents are usually rolled in vanilla-scented confectioners' sugar to coat them entirely, or the tips are dipped in melted chocolate (as in Ella's recipe).

An apocryphal legend says that these crescent-shaped cookies were invented in Vienna in 1683, when the city was under siege by Ottoman Turkish forces. Supposedly the bakers of Vienna, who rose early in the morning to make their wares, heard the Turks tunneling under the city walls. The bakers alerted the defenders of Vienna, and the city was saved. In celebration they created a new kind of cookie in the form of the crescent moon depicted on the Turkish flag.

A similar story is told about a baker in Budapest when that city was under siege by the Turks in 1686. But culinary history tells us that pastries made in that shape had been baked in Europe for hundreds of years before the Turks ever threatened the cities of Vienna and Budapest.[20] In earlier times, perhaps the shape was meant to represent animal horns: in Germany today, crescent-shaped cookies made with marzipan and almond flour, rolled in flaked almonds before baking and the tips later dipped in melted chocolate, are known as *Mandelhörnchen* (little almond horns).

Vanilla crescents are often associated with Christmastime, although many pastry shops sell them year-round

155

because they're so popular with customers. Some pastry-shop cafés even serve their coffee with a little vanilla crescent cookie balanced on the saucer next to the cup.

Editor

Orange-Almond Wreath Cookies

Belli Tante's sister, Margaret, gave her this recipe from her own family's heirloom collection. These are especially popular at Christmastime.

▶ NOTE: For this recipe you need both a round, 2-inch diameter (or smaller) scalloped-edge cookie cutter and a round, 2-inch diameter (or smaller) scalloped-edge cookie cutter with a hole in the center (wreath-shaped).

Dough

1 stick (8 tablespoons, 4 ounces, ½ cup) unsalted butter, plus 1 more tablespoon butter, at room temperature
1 cup confectioners' sugar
2 large egg yolks
2 tablespoons finely grated orange zest

Egg wash

1 egg white
½ teaspoon water
2 ounces slivered almonds, toasted and finely chopped

Assembly

Orange marmalade or apricot jam

▶ Preheat the oven to 325°F. Butter and flour two large cookie sheets, or line them with parchment paper.

▶ **Dough:** Beat the butter with the sugar in the bowl of a stand mixer with the paddle attachment until well combined. Add the egg yolks one at a time, beating just until well mixed, then beat in the orange zest. Gradually add the flour, scraping down the sides of the bowl as needed. Do not overbeat.

● Roll out the dough on a well-floured surface to a thickness of ⅛ inch. Dip the cookie cutters in flour, shaking off the excess. Cut out an equal number of solid circles and wreath-shaped circles (with a hole in the center). Gather up the dough scraps and press them together into a ball, then roll and cut again to make a total of 24 solid circles and 24 with a hole in them.

▶ **Egg wash:** Place the circles of dough on prepared cookie sheets, 1 inch apart, and lightly brush each with the egg-white mixture. Sprinkle finely chopped almonds over *only* the cookies that have a hole in the center.

- Bake on the middle rack of the oven (one baking sheet at a time) at 325°F for 12 to 14 minutes, or until cookies are lightly browned around the edges. Remove cookies from the pan and let them cool on a wire rack.

▶ **Assembly:** When the cookies are completely cool, spread the jam over the entire top of the solid cookies and place a wreath-shaped cookie on top of the jam, so the jam shows through the hole.

▶ Makes 24 pretty wreath cookies.

Ella teaching her grandson Russell to make cookies in her kitchen.

Meringue-and-Raspberry
Sandwich Cookies

A dear Hungarian friend of mine gave me this recipe while I was visiting her in Sarasota, Florida. Generations of her family have enjoyed these pretty little cookies, as I'm sure your family will too. You can also make them with apricot jam if you prefer.

Dough

2 sticks (16 tablespoons, 8 ounces, 1 cup) unsalted butter, at room temperature
4 cups all-purpose flour, sifted
3 large eggs yolks (reserve the whites)
½ cup granulated sugar
Finely grated zest of 1 lemon
¼ cup ice water

Meringue

3 large egg whites
Pinch of salt
⅓ cup granulated sugar
A few drops of fresh lemon juice

Assembly

Seedless raspberry jam (or apricot jam)

▶ Preheat the oven to 350°F. Line two large cookie sheets with parchment paper. Butter the paper and underneath the corners of the paper so that the paper sticks to the cookie sheet.

▶ Dough: In a medium bowl, combine flour and butter, using your fingers or a pastry blender to make a mixture resembling coarse breadcrumbs.

• In another bowl beat the egg yolks with sugar for 2 minutes with a handheld mixer. Add the egg-yolk mixture to the flour mixture.

Stir in the lemon zest. Knead the ingredients together, drizzling in ice water, one tablespoon at a time, to make soft dough. Form it into two equal size balls, then flatten them a little to form disks. Wrap them in plastic wrap and let the dough rest in the refrigerator for about 30 minutes.

- Place a large piece of parchment paper on a work surface and dust it generously with flour. Roll out the first disk of dough until it is about ⅛ inch thick. Cut out cookies using a 2-inch-diameter round cookie cutter. Use a small spatula to lift the cut-out dough onto the prepared cookie sheets, spacing them evenly apart. Place about 12 to 15 rounds of dough on each cookie sheet.

▶ **Meringue:** Using a handheld mixer, beat the egg whites with salt until soft peaks form. With the mixer at medium speed, add the sugar, one tablespoon at a time, then the lemon juice. Increase the speed to high, and beat until the meringue becomes stiff but still glossy, not dry.

- Cover the cut-out dough pieces on *one* cookie sheet with dollops of meringue, spreading it evenly over the dough (or pipe the meringue onto the dough with the fine star tip on a pastry bag). Bake on the middle rack of the oven at 350°F for 12 to 15 minutes, or until the meringue feels firm to the touch and the cookies are lightly golden-brown around the edges. Let the cookies cool on the pan set on a wire rack.

- Bake the cut-out dough on the other cookie sheet (with no meringue on them) on the middle rack of the oven at 350°F for 10 to 15 minutes, or until the cookies are light golden-brown. Let them cool on the pan set on a wire rack.

▶ **Assembly:** Spread the jam on one side of the plain cookies and sandwich each with the bottom of the cookies covered with meringue. (The jam-sandwiched cookie rounds will be on the bottom, with the baked meringue on top.) Enjoy immediately, or store in an airtight container.

▶ Makes 40 cookies.

Hungarian Almond Biscotti

My husband's cousin, Gyopár Szarka, served these biscotti to us at a family gathering in Budapest, where we sat on her terrace overlooking the Danube River. These Hungarian-style biscotti are delicate, wafer-thin slices, not at all like the thick Italian biscotti. Keep them in a cookie jar to have on hand as a snack or to serve when unexpected guests arrive.

▶ **ADVANCE PREPARATION AND SPECIAL EQUIPMENT:** This recipe is made in two stages, on separate days, so plan your timing accordingly. You will need a German *Rehrucken* loaf pan, a long, tunnel-shaped pan (sometimes called a half-round mold) available at specialty kitchenware shops or by mail order. The dough needs to be refrigerated for 24 hours before slicing.

4 large egg whites
½ cup granulated sugar
½ teaspoon baking powder
1 cup plus 1 tablespoon all-purpose flour
1½ cups (7½ ounces) whole unblanched almonds

▶ Preheat the oven to 350°F. Heavily butter and flour a *Rehrucken* mold, shaking out the excess flour.

▶ **First day:** Using a handheld mixer, beat the egg whites with the sugar in a medium bowl until stiff peaks form. In a separate bowl, mix the baking powder with the flour. With the mixer on low speed, slowly add the flour mixture to the egg whites, then beat for 1 minute longer. Fold the whole almonds into the dough.

 • Pour this mixture into the prepared baking pan. Bake on the middle rack of the oven at 350°F for 5 minutes. Reduce the heat to 300°F and bake for an additional 25 minutes, or until the top is firm to the touch.

 • Wet a clean cotton kitchen towel and wring out the excess water so the towel is damp. As soon as the pan is removed from the oven, immediately remove the baked dough from the pan and wrap it in the damp towel. Refrigerate dough wrapped this way for at least 24 hours.

▶ **Second day:** Preheat the oven to 325°F. Use a serrated knife to slice the loaf crosswise into wafer-thin slices and place them on a baking sheet. Bake at 325°F for 5 minutes. Reduce the heat to 275°F and bake for an additional 10 minutes. Turn over the biscotti and bake about 5 minutes longer, until they turn a light golden-brown color.

- Let the biscotti cool on the pan set on a wire rack. These biscotti will be crisp. To store, place between sheets of wax paper in a cookie jar or tightly sealed plastic container.

▶ Makes about 40 Hungarian biscotti.

Hungarian Almond Biscotti are thinner than their Italian namesakes.

Hungarian Almond Tea Pastries

Serve these pastry squares with your afternoon tea or coffee, at a children's party, or at your church or synagogue functions. This treat can be made in advance and frozen in an airtight plastic bag, so you'll have this nice pastry to offer your guests at any time.

1¾ sticks (14 tablespoons, 7 ounces) unsalted butter, at room temperature
1 cup granulated sugar
4 large egg yolks, at room temperature
Finely grated zest of 1 large lemon
4 large egg whites, at room temperature
Pinch of salt
1⅓ cups all-purpose flour
½ cup blanched or unblanched whole almonds, toasted and finely chopped*
2 tablespoons confectioners' sugar
⅓ cup slivered blanched and toasted almonds, for decorations
* Toast whole almonds (blanched or unblanched) in a preheated 350 F oven for 8 to 10 minutes. Let cool, then finely chop before measuring.

▶ Preheat the oven to 325°F. Line the bottom of an 8 × 12–inch baking pan with a piece of parchment. Butter the paper and sides of the pan. Sprinkle with flour, shaking off the excess.

▶ In the bowl of a stand mixer fitted with the paddle attachment, beat the butter and sugar together for 5 minutes on medium speed. Add the egg yolks one at a time and continue beating until mixture is light yellow in color. Add lemon zest and beat it for 1 minute longer.

• Using a handheld electric mixer, beat the egg whites with a pinch of salt until stiff peaks form. Fold the flour into the butter-sugar mixture and then gradually fold in the egg whites.

• Pour the batter into the prepared baking pan, spreading it evenly with a spatula.

- Mix the finely chopped almonds with the confectioners' sugar in a small bowl and sprinkle this evenly over top of the batter, lightly pressing it into the dough. Then press the slivered almonds vertically in rows into the dough, with the top of the almonds sticking out of the dough.

- Bake on the middle rack of the oven at 325°F for about 40 minutes, until a toothpick inserted into the pastry comes out clean. Let the pastry cool in the baking pan set on a wire rack. Cut it into 2-inch squares.

▶ Makes 24 little almond pastries.

Hungarian Cherry Squares

Known in Hungarian as meggyes pite *(cherry pie), this pastry of fresh cherries sandwiched between short-crust dough is one of my favorite spring-time desserts. When I came home from college for spring break, this is what my mother always greeted me with. What a comforting welcome! It's often made with sour cherries, but sweet cherries are just as good in this pastry, which is cut into diamond shapes or squares for serving.*

Dough

3 cups all-purpose flour
¼ teaspoon baking powder
2½ tablespoons confectioners' sugar
1 teaspoon salt
2 sticks (16 tablespoons, 8 ounces, 1 cup) unsalted butter, cut into ½-inch cubes and chilled
1 tablespoon finely grated lemon zest
3 large egg yolks
3 tablespoons sour cream
½ cup ice water
⅓ cup almond flour (made from ¼ cup whole almonds)
5 vanilla wafer or butter cookies crushed into crumbs

Filling

½ cup granulated sugar
1 teaspoon finely grated lemon zest
4 cups pitted fresh cherries or sour cherries, or a combination of the two kinds

Egg wash

1 large egg yolk
½ teaspoon water

Garnish

Confectioners' sugar

▶ Preheat the oven to 325°F. Butter the bottom of a 10 × 15–inch baking pan. Line with parchment paper. Butter the paper and sides of the pan. Sprinkle with flour, shaking off the excess.

▶ **Dough:** Whisk the flour, baking powder, confectioners' sugar, and salt together in a large mixing bowl. Add the butter and work it into the dry ingredients with your fingers or using a pastry cutter to make a coarse meal. Sprinkle in the lemon zest and work it into the dough.

- In a separate bowl, beat the eggs with a fork and mix in the sour cream. Add this to the dough and mix well together. Add the ice water, mixing with your hands to make soft dough.

- Divide the dough into two round balls, then flatten them to form a disk. Sprinkle your work surface with flour. Lightly knead each disk by hand, then form the dough again into two equal-size disks. Wrap the dough in plastic wrap and refrigerate for a couple of hours.

- Roll out each dough disc into a 10 × 15–inch rectangle. Place the first rectangle of dough on the bottom of the prepared baking pan, spreading the pastry by hand all the way to the sides. Sprinkle the almond flour and vanilla wafer crumbs evenly over the dough.

▶ **Filling:** Combine the sugar, lemon zest, and cherries in a large bowl. Pour this mixture on top of the dough and spread it evenly, leaving about ½ inch of the dough uncovered all around. Cover the cherries with the second sheet of dough and seal the pastry around the edges by pressing the two layers of dough together. Prick the top of the dough at 1-inch intervals with fork.

Hungarian Cherry Squares.

▶ **Egg wash:** Whisk together the egg yolk and water. Brush this on top of the pastry. Bake on the middle rack of the oven at 325°F for 35 to 40 minutes. The *pite* should be golden brown on the top. Let it cool in the pan set on a wire rack.

▶ **Garnish:** When cool, cut it into diamond shapes, 1½ × 3–inch rectangular bars, or 2-inch squares. Sift confectioners' sugar lightly over the top before serving.

▶ Makes approximately 32 pieces.

HUNGARIAN PITÉK

Hungarian *piték* are sweet pastries that lie between cakes and pies on the culinary scale—although most Americans would consider them more pie than cake. *Piték* are favorite homestyle treats, easy to make and filling to eat. They're especially well loved snacks for kids. *Piték* are also made by professional bakers because adults like these pastries so much, too, especially with midmorning or afternoon coffee at a pastry shop or coffeehouse.

Pastry dough made with flour, sugar, and butter or lard is rolled out to fit into a flat, rimmed baking sheet. Often a sweet filling is spread over all the dough, then a top layer of dough is added before the *pite* is baked. Favorite fillings include grated apples with walnuts, raisins, and cinnamon; fresh white farmers' cheese with sour cream and sugar; and sour or sweet cherries (or a mixture of the two) with sugar and cinnamon. Occasionally a latticework top crust is used, especially for cherry *pite*.

Sometimes the bottom layer of dough is partially baked, then spread with a sweet, fluffy meringue containing finely chopped or ground walnuts, hazelnuts, or almonds, and the *pite* is baked again (without a top crust) until the meringue is lightly browned. *Piték* are customarily cut into squares or diamond shapes for serving and garnished with a dusting of confectioners' sugar.

Editor

Walnut Diamonds

This recipe from Belli Tante's heirloom collection has been handed down through several generations. It is as popular today as it was a century ago.

Bottom layer

3 sticks (24 tablespoons, 12 ounces, 1½ cups) unsalted butter, at room temperature

1 cup granulated sugar

½ cup freshly squeezed lemon juice (approximately 3 lemons; zest 2 lemons before squeezing, to use for top layer)

6 large eggs, separated (use the 6 yolks for the bottom layer, and the 6 whites for the top layer)

4 cups all-purpose flour

½ teaspoon baking powder

¼ teaspoon salt

One 12-ounce jar (or 1¼ cups) of apricot jam or sour-cherry jam

Top layer

6 large egg whites (from above), at room temperature

1 cup confectioners' sugar

3 cups walnut flour or finely chopped walnuts (made from about 10 ounces or 3 cups of walnuts)

Finely grated zest of 2 lemons

Garnish

Confectioners' sugar

▶ Preheat the oven to 350°F. Butter an 11 × 17–inch rimmed baking sheet. Line with parchment paper, then butter the paper and sides of the pan. Sprinkle with flour, shaking off the excess.

▶ **Bottom layer:** In the bowl of a stand mixer fitted with the paddle attachment, beat the butter and the sugar on medium speed until light and smooth, about 5 minutes. Add the lemon juice, then add the egg yolks, one by one, beating at medium speed until well blended.

- In a medium bowl, mix together the flour, baking powder, and salt. With the mixer on low speed, add this to the butter-and-egg mixture, ½ cup at a time. Beat for about 2 minutes, until the dough becomes smooth.

- Drop small portions of the dough into the prepared pan, then even out the dough by pressing it down with your fingers to make a smooth layer of dough filling the bottom of the pan. Spread the jam evenly over this layer.

▶ **Top layer:** In a clean bowl of a stand mixer fitted with the whisk attachment, beat the egg whites at high speed until they form soft peaks. Slowly add the confectioners' sugar, beating until stiff, glossy peaks form. Fold in the walnuts and lemon zest. Spread this mixture evenly on top of the apricot jam.

- Bake on the middle rack of the oven at 350°F for about 40 minutes, then cut a small piece from a corner. If the bottom is lightly browned, it is done. If not, cover the pan with foil and bake an additional 5 to 10 minutes. Cool in the pan set on a wire rack.

▶ **Garnish:** To serve, cut around the edges of the pan, then cut the pastry on the diagonal into 1 × 1½–inch diamonds, or into 1 × 1½–inch bars, or into squares. Sift confectioners' sugar over the tops before serving.

- Store in a tightly covered container, layered between sheets of parchment or wax paper. These can also be frozen in a tightly covered container.

▶ Makes about 60 delicious little pastry bars.

HUNGARIAN APRICOTS

Apricots have been grown in Hungary for more than five hundred years, in private gardens and large plantations, their pretty pink-and-white blossoms announcing the arrival of spring. But the systematic cultivation of apricot orchards in Hungary has waxed and waned over the centuries, for a number of reasons. In the nineteenth century, however, large apricot orchards were planted in the sandy soils of the flat plain between the Danube and Tisza Rivers, to prevent soil erosion from the winds. And today, the largest quantity and best quality of apricots are still grown on the Great Plain of Hungary, especially in the area around the city of Kecskemét in the center of the country.[21]

Apricots are an important fruit in Hungarian cuisine. In addition to being eaten fresh, they're preserved by being dried, simmered with sugar to make jam, and cooked very slowly, with or without sugar, to make a thick paste known as *lekvar*, a kind of apricot butter that is used in baking and also as a spread for bread.

Apricots are an ingredient in many Hungarian sweets, from cakes and cookies to pies and other pastries. Apricot jam is used as a filling or topping for elegant tortes. Apricot dumplings are a favorite Hungarian treat, eaten as a main dish and as a dessert. Each large dumpling is made from a whole, pitted apricot encased in a flour-and-potato dough, boiled until done, then rolled in dry bread crumbs, garnished with melted butter, and liberally sprinkled with confectioners' sugar. And clear, potent apricot brandy from Kecskemét is especially appreciated by connoisseurs for its rich aroma and smooth taste, made by distilling the alcohol from apricot pulp and crushed apricot kernels.

Editor

Sweet Cheese-and-Noodle Pie (Vargabéles)

Vargabéles is a traditional Transylvanian dessert, a double-crust pie made of puff pastry (or layers of strudel dough) with a filling of fresh pasta combined with fresh white farmers' cheese, sour cream, lemon zest, and raisins. In earlier times Hungarian cooks made the fresh pasta at home. They also laboriously rolled out more dough into very thin sheets, then brushed them with melted butter as they stacked them up to make several layers for the pie crust. Today this treat is much easier to make with store-bought fresh (or dried) pasta and good-quality frozen puff pastry sheets. Just be sure to buy a brand of puff pastry made with butter.

Pie crust

1 box (18 ounces) frozen puff pastry sheets

Filling

Pinch of salt
9 ounces fresh fettuccine pasta (or 7 ounces dry fettuccine pasta)
1¼ cups granulated sugar
7 large eggs, separated, at room temperature
¾ stick (6 tablespoons, 3 ounces) unsalted butter, at room temperature
1 cup sour cream, at room temperature
2 cups golden raisins
2 pounds small-curd, full-fat cottage cheese (very well drained of excess moisture), at room temperature, pressed through a sieve*
2 tablespoons vanilla extract
Finely grated zest of 1½ large lemons
*Don't use creamed cottage cheese, which is too moist. You can also use 2 pounds of farmers' cheese or pot cheese, at room temperature, pressed through a sieve.

Assembly

Melted butter

172

Garnish

Confectioners' sugar

▶ **Pie crust:** Take the puff pastry sheets out of the wrapping and let them thaw for 20 minutes. Then open out the pastry sheets, and let them thaw for an additional 10 minutes.

▶ **Filling:** Meanwhile, bring 8 cups of water to boil in a large pot. Add the pinch of salt and the pasta. Cook the pasta for 4 minutes (longer if using dried pasta), then drain in a colander and rinse with cold water. Drain thoroughly, and chop the pasta into pieces about 2 inches long.

• In a large bowl, combine the granulated sugar, 7 egg yolks, butter, sour cream, raisins, cottage cheese, vanilla extract, and lemon zest. Blend together with a spatula. Add the chopped pasta and mix well.

• Beat the 7 egg whites in a large bowl until stiff peaks form, then fold them into the cottage-cheese mixture.

▶ Preheat the oven to 375°F. Line an 11 × 17–inch jelly-roll pan with parchment paper. Butter the paper and sprinkle with flour, shaking off the excess.

▶ **Assembly:** On a very well-floured surface, roll out the pastry sheets into two 11 × 17–inch rectangles. Place one pastry sheet in the prepared baking pan. Spread the filling on top, leaving about ½ inch of the dough uncovered all around. Top with the second pastry sheet. Brush the edges of the dough with water and pinch them together to seal. Brush the top with melted butter.

• Bake on a rack in the lowest position in the oven at 375°F for 30 minutes or until the top turns golden brown. Cool completely in the pan set on a wire rack.

▶ **Garnish:** To serve, sift confectioners' sugar over the top, and cut into 3 × 2–inch rectangles.

▶ Makes about 20 small pastries.

HUNGARIAN FARMERS' CHEESE

Known as *túrós* in Hungarian—and farmers' cheese or pot cheese in English—this is a type of fresh, soft white cheese with very small curds, usually made from cows' milk. It's used in many Hungarian recipes, savory and sweet. For sweet dishes *túrós* is often combined with raisins and flavored with lemon zest and vanilla.

You can purchase farmers' cheese at many delicatessens, Eastern European food stores, and major supermarkets in the United States, where it is usually packaged in 1-pound (16-ounce) blocks wrapped in wax paper or packed into tubs. Farmers' cheese is produced with different levels of fat content, from no fat to full fat. For most Hungarian recipes, full-fat is recommended.

Farmers' cheese is not the same as cottage cheese in America, which is softer, more moist, and has larger curds. Occasionally dry-curd (not creamed) cottage cheese can be substituted for farmers' cheese in a recipe, if the cottage cheese is well drained of excess moisture and pressed through a sieve before using.

Editor

Gerbeaud Slices

In the Hungarian baking repertoire there are many versions of this well-known pastry, whose name comes from the famous Gerbeaud pastry shop in Budapest. A recipe from the family collection of my friend Judith Schultze inspired my own recipe here. Every Christmas we enjoyed this traditional time-tested treat at Judith's holiday gatherings.

Dough

5 cups all-purpose flour
¼ cup confectioners' sugar
1 teaspoon salt
1 tablespoon baking powder
4½ sticks (36 tablespoons, 18 ounces, 2¼ cups) unsalted butter, at room temperature
8 large egg yolks
2 tablespoons sour cream, at room temperature

Filling

3 cups walnut flour (from about 10 ounces or 3 cups of walnuts)
2 cups granulated sugar
One-half of an 9-ounce jar (or 1 cup) of apricot preserves

Chocolate glaze

5 ounces semi-sweet chocolate, finely chopped
5 tablespoons unsalted butter, at room temperature
¼ cup light corn syrup

▶ Preheat the oven to 350°F. Line a 10 × 15–inch jelly-roll pan with parchment paper. Butter the parchment and sides of the pan. Sprinkle with flour, shaking off the excess. Cut 3 pieces of parchment paper each 10 × 15 inches and set aside.

▶ **Dough:** In a large bowl, whisk together the flour, confectioners' sugar, salt, and baking powder. Add the butter, using your fingers or a pastry blender to work the butter into the flour until it is well incorporated.

- In another bowl beat the egg yolks with a fork, add the sour cream, and beat until it is well incorporated. Add this to the flour mixture, mixing it first with a large spoon, then kneading by hand. At first the dough will be sticky, but after about 5 minutes of kneading it will become smooth. Divide the dough into three equal-size balls, then flatten each into a disk. Let them rest for 15 minutes at room temperature.

▶ **Filling:** Whisk the walnut flour and sugar together in a medium bowl.

▶ **Assembly:** Sprinkle one sheet of 10 × 15–inch parchment paper with flour. Place the first disk on it and roll it out to the shape and size of the parchment paper. Lift up the paper with the dough on it, turn it over, and place the dough on the buttered parchment paper in the prepared pan. Remove the top piece of parchment paper. Spread half of the apricot jam on the dough. Sprinkle half of the walnut-and-sugar mixture on top.

- Roll out the second disk of dough on another 10 × 15–inch piece of parchment paper. Turn the dough over and place it in the pan on top of the dough covered with the apricot jam and walnut mixture. Remove the top piece of parchment paper. Spread the remaining apricot jam evenly on top and sprinkle it with the other half of the walnut-and-sugar mixture.

- Roll out the third disk of dough on the remaining piece of parchment paper. Turn it over and place the dough on top of the ingredients in the pan. Remove the top piece of parchment paper. Prick the top layer in several places with a fork, about fifteen times.

- Bake on the middle rack of the oven at 350°F for 30 to 40 minutes, until the top is golden-brown in color. Let it cool in the pan set on a wire rack for 30 minutes.

▶ **Chocolate glaze:** Finely chop or grate the chocolate and place in the top pan of a metal double boiler. Fill the bottom pan with some water. Check to see that when the upper pan is placed on top, the water does not touch it, then set the top pan aside. When the water has come to a boil, remove from the heat and place the pan with the chocolate on top. Stir until the chocolate is smooth. Combine the butter and corn syrup in a small saucepan over very low heat. Add the chocolate, mixing until glaze is smooth.

- Let the chocolate mixture cool to lukewarm, then pour the chocolate glaze on top of the baked dough and smooth it with a spatula. Cover and refrigerate for 4 hours or overnight. Cut it into 1½-inch squares or 1 × 1½–inch rectangular pieces.

▶ Makes approximately 40 slices.

GERBEAUD IN BUDAPEST

Gerbeaud is surely the most famous coffeehouse–pastry shop in Budapest, known for more than 150 years for the high quality of its coffees, cakes, tortes, and candies, and also for its innovations in pastry making and confectionery.

The business was started by Henrik Kugler as a confectionery store in 1858 and in 1870 moved to its current location in the city center, on a fashionable square near the Danube River. There Kugler opened an elegant establishment that attracted the elite of Budapest society, as well as leading politicians and visiting celebrities. In 1884 the business passed to his associate, a Swiss pastry chef, Emil Gerbeaud, who expanded the number of products for sale, both on-site and for takeout in pretty boxes. In 1919 he also upgraded the décor, installing marble floors, countertops, and tabletops; cherry wood cabinetry, plush upholstery, and brocade drapery; and an ornate stucco ceiling hung with crystal chandeliers.

Gerbeaud's coffeehouse survived two world wars, nationalization by the state in 1949, the Hungarian Uprising of 1956, and decline under the Communist regime between 1948 and 1989. In 1995 it was bought by a German businessman who restored the interior to its former glory, and whose confectioners continue to develop new taste treats for their customers today.[22]

The Gerbeaud Slice is one of the shop's pastry creations that has remained popular for decades. The classic recipe consists of three thin layers of a sweet dough made with a small amount of yeast, alternating with layers of thick apricot jam liberally sprinkled with ground walnuts, and a smooth chocolate glaze on top. Baked in a large flat pan, the rich pastry is then cut into rectangular bars for serving.

Gerbeaud Slices are so beloved by Hungarians that they're also baked by home cooks, many of whom have developed their own personal variations on the original recipe. And whether homemade or store-bought, Gerbeaud Slices are always considered traditional for Hungarian wedding receptions.

Editor

Gerbeaud's elegant pastry shop in Budapest in the nineteenth century, when it was still owned by the original founder, Henrik Kugler.

CAKES

▶ **NOTE:** In these recipes, volume measurements of *nut flours* (in cups) are an approximation, to the nearest fraction of a cup, based on grinding the amount of *whole nuts* listed in the recipe. Volume measurements of nut flours can vary slightly, depending on the size of the nuts and the method used for grinding them. Since hand-ground nut flours are fluffier and less dense than store-bought nut flours, the volume of hand-ground nut flour can be slightly larger than the volume of store-bought nut flour, even though they both weigh the same. Likewise, tortes made with commercially ground nut flours tend to be a bit denser than those made with nuts ground by hand.

For best results measure out the amount of *whole nuts* needed in a recipe (in cups, or by weight in ounces), then grind them in your own kitchen and use the amount of nut flour that you produce. If using *store-bought nut flour,* then use the number of cups of *nut flour* specified in the recipe.

Orange Kugelhopf

Kugelhopf is a very well-known cake in Hungary and Austria. Some culinary historians say that it was Emperor Franz Joseph I's favorite breakfast cake. The orange-wine custard is a garnishing sauce. This cake is nice to serve with your afternoon coffee or tea or as a special treat for a bridal shower.

▶ **NOTE:** For this recipe you need a special *Kugelhopf* pan, a round cake mold with fluted edges and a tube in the middle. You can also use a Bundt pan.

Yeast sponge

1 tablespoon active dry yeast
½ teaspoon sugar
¼ cup lukewarm milk (105–115°F)
2 teaspoons all-purpose flour

Cake

1 stick (8 tablespoons, 4 ounces, ½ cup) unsalted butter, at room temperature
2 cups confectioners' sugar
Pinch of salt
5 large egg yolks
1 tablespoon orange extract or orange liqueur
3 cups all-purpose flour
¾ cup whole milk
Finely grated zest of 2 medium navel oranges
2 medium navel oranges, peeled and cut into ½-inch pieces
2 tablespoons melted unsalted butter (for the *Kugelhopf* or Bundt pan)
Enough whole blanched almonds for 1 almond in each depression at the bottom of the *Kugelhopf* or Bundt pan

Orange-wine custard

¾ cup dry white wine, preferably Chablis

4 large egg yolks
1 large egg
¾ cup granulated sugar
Finely grated zest of 1 medium navel orange

Garnish

Confectioners' sugar

▶ **Yeast sponge:** Dissolve the yeast and sugar in the warm milk. Mix well. Sprinkle the top with flour. Let rise for 5 minutes in a warm place.

▶ **Cake:** In the bowl of a stand mixer fitted with the paddle attachment, beat the butter with the confectioners' sugar and salt for 1 minute on low speed with a tea towel covering the mixer (so the sugar won't fly out), then on high speed for 3 minutes, until the mixture is light in color and texture. Add the egg yolks one at a time while continuing to beat. Add the orange extract (or orange liqueur), flour, and yeast sponge. Beat on low speed for 10 minutes. Add enough milk to make semifirm dough. Add the orange zest, then stop beating. Fold in the orange pieces.

• Butter a 9½-inch-diameter *Kugelhopf* pan or 9-inch-diameter Bundt pan.

• Place 1 whole almond in each of the fluted depressions in the bottom of the *Kugelhopf* mold or Bundt pan. Press the dough into the mold.

• Cover the cake mold with a kitchen towel and let the dough rise in a warm, draft-free place for 2 hours, or until it is double in size.

• About 20 minutes before baking, while the batter is still rising, position a rack in the lower third of the oven and preheat to 350°F.

• Bake on the lower rack of the oven at 350°F for 40 to 45 minutes, or until the top is golden-brown in color. Cool in the pan set on a wire rack.

▶ **Orange-wine custard:** Pour the wine into the top of a metal double boiler set over, but not touching, simmering water. Keep the water simmering until the wine is warm.

- Using a handheld mixer, beat the egg yolks and whole egg with the sugar in a medium bowl for 2 minutes. Continue beating at medium speed while you drizzle the warm wine into the egg mixture. Then beat for 1 more minute.

- Pour this mixture back into the top pan of the double boiler and set it over the simmering water. Beat until it begins to thicken. Then stop beating and immediately remove the top pan from the heat and place it in a larger bowl of ice water. Beat the custard over the ice water so it cools down and stops cooking. Mix in the orange zest, let the custard cool completely, and then refrigerate for 2 hours.

▶ **Garnish:** Invert the cake onto a serving plate. (The whole almonds will be baked onto the top of the cake.) Dust the cake generously with confectioners' sugar. Cut the cake into 1½-inch slices and serve with 4 tablespoons of custard spooned over each slice, or pooled on the dessert plate around each cake slice.

▶ Makes 10 to 12 servings.

Kugelhopf is a popular type of cake throughout central Europe.

KUGELHOPF/GUGELHUPF

Kugelhopf and *Gugelhupf* are the interchangeable names for two very different kinds of cakes that are made across the middle of Europe, from the French region of Alsace to the lands of the former Austro-Hungarian Empire (where *Gugelhupf* is the more common spelling). Both are baked in a special cake mold—round with fluted sides, nearly as tall as it is wide, and with a slender tube in the center extending from bottom to top. A popular legend says that cakes in this shape resembling a Turk's turban were created by Austrian bakers to celebrate the Habsburg victory over the Ottoman Turks outside the walls of Vienna in 1683. But molds of this shape were already being made in Roman times, and recipes for *Kugelhopf/Gugelhupf* date back to medieval Austria or even earlier.[23]

Some of the cakes baked in these distinctive molds are made from a yeast-raised dough, producing a light-textured cake much like a sweet bread. Others are based on a sponge-cake batter lightened by beaten eggs. And still others are leavened with baking powder. The yeast-raised versions (as in Ella Szabó's recipe) are considered to be the older, original type, since yeast was used as a leavening agent long before baking powder made its way into kitchens.

Kugelhopf/Gugelhupf is well loved in Austria, where it's eaten throughout the day, year-round, from breakfast to afternoon coffee time. Central European cookbooks provide dozens of different recipes for *Kugelhopf/Gugelhupf*. Coffeehouses and pastry shops offer several different flavor choices. And this tasty cake also appears on the bread table at almost every Austrian hotel's breakfast buffet.

Editor

Russian Cream Torte

At pastry shops throughout Hungary, this is a well-loved torte, its cream filling flavored with candied orange peel and rum-soaked currants. It's worth making at home, too. As beautiful as it is flavorful, this torte is a lovely addition to any party or special event. But you need to start preparing this torte two days in advance, so plan ahead.

▶ **ADVANCE PREPARATION:** The candied orange peel and rum-soaked currants need to be made 12 to 24 hours before you make the cake filling.

Candied orange peel

1 medium orange
1 cup water
½ cup sugar

Currants

½ cup currants (or dark raisins, chopped)
½ cup dark rum

Cake layers

7 large eggs
⅓ cup plus 1 tablespoon granulated sugar
½ cup plus 1 tablespoon all-purpose flour
1 teaspoon baking powder

Filling

1 envelope unflavored gelatin
2 tablespoons water
4 large egg yolks
2 cups whole milk
1 cup heavy whipping cream
½ cup granulated sugar

Assembly

¾ cup dark rum

Garnish

2 cups heavy whipping cream, very cold
3 tablespoons confectioners' sugar

▶ **Candied orange peel:** Cut all the peel off the orange in strips about 1/2-inch wide, leaving behind the white pith between the peel and the orange's flesh. Combine the orange peel with the water and sugar in a small saucepan. Bring to a boil, then simmer for 10 minutes. Remove from the heat. Let the peel sit overnight in the sugar syrup.

▶ **Currants:** In a small bowl, soak the currants or raisins overnight in rum.

▶ **The next day:** Preheat the oven to 375°F. Butter a 10-inch-round springform pan and line the bottom with parchment paper. Butter and flour the paper and sides of the pan. Sprinkle with flour, shaking off the excess.

▶ **Cake layers:** In the bowl of a stand mixer fitted with the whisk attachment, beat the eggs with the sugar on high speed until the mixture has tripled in volume and resembles whipped cream (about 10 minutes). In a separate bowl whisk together the flour and baking powder. Add this flour mixture, 1 tablespoonful at a time, to the egg mixture while beating on low speed. Spread batter evenly in the prepared springform pan.

- Bake at 375°F for about 30 minutes, until a toothpick inserted into the center of the cake comes out clean. The top of the cake should be lightly toasted in color and should spring back when touched.

- Let the cake cool in the pan for 1 hour, set on a wire rack.

▶ **Filling:** Dissolve the gelatin in 2 tablespoons of lukewarm water in a small bowl. Set aside.

- Whisk together the egg yolks and milk in a separate bowl, then strain through a sieve into the top pan of a metal double boiler set over, but not touching, simmering water. Cook, stirring constantly, over medium heat until the custard starts to thicken and coats the sides of a spoon (about 3 minutes). Remove from the heat and immediately whisk in the softened gelatin.

- To cool the egg custard, place the pan in a bowl filled with 2 cups of ice and 2 cups of cold water. Stir constantly until the mixture is lukewarm, then remove the pan from the ice-water bath and refrigerate the custard for about 1 hour.

- While the custard is cooling, drain the candied orange peel and chop it into very small pieces. Drain the currants or raisins in a sieve and press gently with a spoon to remove any excess liquid.

- Chill a mixing bowl and mixer whisk attachment in the freezer. Whip the 1 cup of heavy cream to soft peaks in the chilled bowl, gradually adding the ½ cup of granulated sugar. Beat until stiff peaks form. Fold the whipped cream into the cooled custard, then fold in the currants and orange peel.

▶ **Assembly:** Remove the cooled cake from the springform pan. Using a serrated knife, cut the cake horizontally into three layers. Remove the parchment paper from the bottom layer and place it cut side up on a nice serving plate. Sprinkle this layer with 5 tablespoons of dark rum. Spread one-fourth of the cream filling evenly on top. Add the next cake layer, sprinkled with 5 tablespoons of rum, and spread one-fourth of the filling evenly on top. Add the top cake layer, sprinkle with the remaining 2 tablespoons of rum, then cover the top and all sides of the cake with the remaining filling. Refrigerate for 3 hours or overnight. (**Note:** At this point you can also freeze the torte for three months, wrapped securely in plastic wrap.)

▶ **Garnish:** Chill a large mixing bowl and mixer whisk attachment in the freezer. Whip the cream in the chilled bowl to soft peaks, gradually adding the confectioners' sugar. Beat until stiff peak forms.

- Cover the sides of the assembled torte with whipped cream. Spoon the remaining whipped cream into a pastry bag fitted with a star tip and pipe decorations along the top and bottom edges. Refrigerate for 2 hours before serving.

▶ Makes 8 to 10 servings.

RUSSIAN CREAM TORTE

The name of this torte has nothing to do with Russia. A Hungarian pastry chef named Sándor Oroszi is usually credited with creating this creamy layered cake sometime between the two world wars, probably in the 1930s, perhaps at a Budapest coffeehouse called Oroszi Kávéház. The name Oroszi is very close to the Hungarian word for "Russian" (Orosz). So when that name (minus the *i*) became attached to the cake, it became a "Russian" Cream Torte (Oroszkrém torta). Or so the story goes. No one really knows for certain.[24]

Like professional cooks around the world, Hungarian pastry chefs have always tried to create new products that would tempt the taste buds of their customers. Russian Cream Torte combined layers of white sponge cake with alternating layers of vanilla custard cream enhanced with raisins soaked in rum, sometimes with chopped candied fruit peel added, too, and the cake was then covered with sweetened whipped cream and decorated according to the baker's whim. Since layered sponge cakes with cream fillings had already been made for centuries, perhaps it was those rummy raisins or colorful candied fruits that captured the palates of pastry lovers in Budapest nearly one hundred years ago and added Russian Cream Torte to the Hungarian pastry repertoire.

Editor

The King's Torte

My dear friend Judith Eckmayer-Wedow, Belli Tante's daughter, gave me this from the original collection of her favorite chocolate torte recipes. It is probably called "The King's Torte" because wives baked this for special occasions honoring their husbands, the "king" of the household.

Cake layers

6 large eggs, separated, at room temperature
5 tablespoons granulated sugar
4 ounces of semi-sweet chocolate, grated
½ cup all-purpose flour

Chocolate-cream filling

3 large egg yolks
¼ cup granulated sugar
1¼ cups whole milk
4 ounces semi-sweet chocolate, finely grated
1 package unflavored gelatin
3 tablespoons water

Whipped-cream filling

2 cups heavy whipping cream, very cold
¼ cup granulated sugar

Garnish

1 cup finely grated semi-sweet chocolate

▶ Preheat the oven to 300°F. Line the bottoms of three 9-inch-diameter round springform pans with parchment paper. Butter the parchment paper and sides of the pan. Sprinkle with a little flour, shaking out the excess.

▶ **Cake layers:** Using a hand mixer, beat the egg yolks and sugar in a large bowl until pale yellow in color. In the bowl of a stand mixer fitted with the whisk attachment, beat the egg whites until stiff. Mix 3 heaping tablespoons of the beaten egg whites into the beaten egg yolks, to lighten them.

- In small bowl combine the grated chocolate with the ½ cup flour. A heaping tablespoon at a time, gently fold this mixture into the egg yolk mixture, then fold in the remaining beaten egg whites. Divide the batter evenly among the three pans.

- Place all three pans on the middle rack in the oven. Bake for 10 to 15 minutes, until the tops of the cakes are firm to the touch.

▶ **Chocolate-cream filling:** Lightly beat the egg yolks in a medium bowl, then add the sugar and milk. Strain through a sieve into the top of a metal double boiler set over, but not touching, simmering water. Cook, stirring constantly, until the mixture thickens. Remove the pan from the heat. Place the top of the double boiler in a bowl of ice water to stop the cooking. Stir the mixture until lukewarm. Then stir in the grated chocolate.

- Sprinkle the gelatin over the cold water in a small heatproof bowl. Let it sit a few minutes to soften. Then set the bowl in a small pan containing 1 inch of boiling water and heat until the gelatin dissolves and looks clear. Do not stir. Let the gelatin cool a bit, then add to the chocolate-and-egg mixture, mixing thoroughly. Let this mixture cool, but use when it's still spreadable, before it fully sets. (It will finish setting firm on the torte.)

▶ **Whipped-cream filling:** Chill a mixing bowl and mixer whisk attachment in the freezer. Whip the cream in the chilled bowl to soft peaks, gradually adding the granulated sugar. Beat until stiff peaks form.

▶ **Assembly:** Place a 12-inch doily on a serving platter and put the first cake layer on top of the doily. Spread one-fourth of the chocolate cream filling on top, followed by one-fourth of the whipped cream. Sprinkle ⅓ cup of the grated chocolate evenly over the whipped cream, then repeat with the next layer of cake, chocolate cream, whipped cream, and grated chocolate. Add the top cake layer, then spread the top and sides with the remaining chocolate cream filling.

▶ **Garnish:** Use a pastry bag fitted with the star tube to pipe the remaining whipped cream in concentric circles around on the top of the cake and to pipe stars around the bottom edge of the cake. Sprinkle the top with the remaining ⅓ cup of grated chocolate.

▶ Makes 8 servings.

▶ **NOTE:** When adding the whipped cream to each cake layer, you can also fill a pastry bag with one-fourth of the whipped cream and pipe it into concentric circles to fill each layer, instead of just spreading it on the layers.

Cherry Sponge Cake

When I was very young, my family used to bicycle every spring to our cottage outside our hometown near the Tisza River in southern Hungary. When cherry season came, excitement was high as my brother, sister, and I picked all sorts of cherries: sweet ones like Germezdorfi and sour ones like Szentesi Meggy. Then we would bring our overflowing baskets home to my mother to make this cherry sponge cake. We pitted the cherries by hand and laboriously beat the eggs for the batter. Someone would start a fire in the old-fashioned stove. My mother would determine when the oven was warm enough by sticking her hand in to test it, finally declaring with authority that it was ready. All of us eagerly waited for the cake to finish baking and cooling so that finally we could enjoy the fruits of our labor. I still marvel at my mother and women like her who mastered the art of cooking and baking as it was handed down through generations, without the aid of modern appliances. However, this recipe has been adapted to suit the modern cook, so it's now very easy to make in your own kitchen.

Cake

8 large eggs, at room temperature
⅓ cup plus 1 tablespoon granulated sugar
¾ cup plus 1 tablespoon all-purpose flour
1 teaspoon baking powder
2 tablespoons finely grated lemon zest
12 ounces fresh sweet or sour cherries (1½ cups pitted cherries, plus 10 more for decorating)

Garnish

Confectioners' sugar
Whipped cream

▶ Preheat the oven to 325°F. Butter a 10-inch round springform pan, then line the bottom with a sheet of parchment paper. Butter the paper and sides of the pan. Sprinkle with flour, shaking off the excess.

▶ **Cake:** In a *6-quart bowl* of a stand mixer fitted with the whisk attachment, beat the eggs and sugar on high speed for about 10 minutes, until the mixture has tripled in volume and resembles whipped cream.

  - In another bowl whisk the baking powder into the flour. Change to slow speed on the mixer, add the flour, and mix for 1 minute. Add the lemon zest and mix thoroughly. Pour the batter into the pan. Top with 1½ cups pitted cherries. They will sink into the batter as it bakes.

  - Bake on the middle rack of the oven at 325°F for 35 minutes, then place the 10 reserved cherries around the outside edge of the cake. Bake about 10 minutes longer, until a toothpick inserted into the cake comes out clean and the top springs back when touched. As soon as the cake comes out of the oven, sift confectioners' sugar over the top.

  - Let the cake cool in the pan, set on a wire rack, at room temperature for 2 hours. Then remove the cake from the pan and peel off the parchment paper. Place the cake on a serving plate.

▶ **Garnish:** Before serving, dust with additional confectioners' sugar. Serve with a dollop of whipped cream if you like. (**Note:** This cake is best eaten on the same day it is made.)

▶ Makes 8 to 10 servings.

Almond-Flour Cake with Mixed Fruits

I dedicated this fruity almond-flour cake to my dear Hungarian friend Magdalena Kendeffy, who was an excellent cook and baker. She gave me her original recipe, made entirely with wheat flour, which I adapted into a richly flavored almond-flour version. This versatile recipe is easy to make in any season because of the variety of fruits you can use. My favorites are cherries, apples, and quince. Our next-door-neighbor's daughter, Jena, asked me to open a pastry shop in town just so she could buy this cake whenever she wanted!

▶ **NOTE:** This recipe makes two thin, single-layer cakes, each with 2 cups of fresh fruit baked on top. The cakes are baked separately in two 9-inch springform pans.

Cakes

1½ sticks (12 tablespoons, 6 ounces, ¾ cup) unsalted butter, at room temperature
¾ cup granulated sugar
3 large eggs, at room temperature
1 tablespoon pure vanilla extract
1 cup almond flour (made from 3½ ounces or ⅔ cup unblanched almonds)
1⅓ cups all-purpose flour (or King Arthur Gluten Free Measure for Measure Flour)
2½ tablespoons baking powder

Fruit

Select 4 cups of fresh fruit of your choice, or 4 cups of mixed fresh fruits:
Pitted whole cherries, sour or sweet
Pitted Italian plums, halved
Pitted apricots, peeled and thinly sliced
Apples, peeled, cored, and thinly sliced
Pears, peeled, cored, and thinly sliced

Cooked quince, cut into slices (see pg. 147)
Blueberries

Garnish

Confectioners' sugar

▶ Preheat the oven to 325°F. Line the bottom of two 9-inch-diameter round springform pans with parchment paper. Butter the paper and the sides of the pan. Sprinkle with flour and shake off the excess.

▶ **Cakes:** In the bowl of a stand mixer fitted with the paddle attachment, beat the butter and the sugar at medium speed until light and fluffy, about 5 minutes. Add the eggs one at a time, beating until each egg is well combined. Add the vanilla and continue to beat for another 10 minutes.

- In another bowl whisk together the almond flour, all-purpose flour, and baking powder. Gradually add this mixture into the butter and eggs, mixing until well combined.

▶ **Fruit:** Fill each springform pan with half of the batter. Smooth the top of the batter, then arrange half the fruit in circles on top of the batter in each pan, closely spacing the pieces together. Press lightly into the batter.

- Bake the cakes together on the middle rack of the oven at 325°F for about 30 minutes, or until a toothpick or skewer inserted into the center comes out clean. Let the cakes cool in the pan set on a wire rack, then refrigerate until needed.

▶ **Garnish:** Before serving, remove the cakes from the pans and sift confectioners' sugar lightly over the cake tops.

▶ Makes 2 cakes, 8 servings each.

HUNGARIAN PLUMS

In addition to foraging for wild plums, Hungarians have a long tradition of cultivating plums on their land. Over several centuries at least twenty varieties of plums have been grown in home gardens, small orchards, and large commercial plantations in Hungary. Today the most important areas for plum cultivation are in the south-central and extreme northeastern parts of the country.

In early spring the trees put forth pink, white, or purple blossoms, depending on the variety of plum, and the fruit is harvested from late June until mid-September. Up to a quarter of the Hungarian plum crop is exported to other countries. The rest is eaten fresh by Hungarians, dried into prunes, used in cooking, and distilled into a potent fruit brandy that is a popular alcoholic drink in Hungary.

Plums, both fresh and dried, are used in many Hungarian dishes. Plums are stewed with cinnamon, cloves, lemon, and sugar to make a filling for fruit tarts and a compote to serve over ice cream. They are pureed and cooked very slowly over low heat to make dark, thick prune butter that is spread over bread, used in baking, and used as the filling for sweet, ravioli-like pasta garnished with cinnamon and confectioners' sugar. Ripe, juicy, pitted plums are stuffed with a sugar cube and encased in a potato dough to make sweet boiled dumplings that are then rolled in breadcrumbs, fried in butter, and served with a dusting of confectioners' sugar. Fresh plums are preserved in spiced red wine or spiced vinegar to accompany roasted turkey at Christmastime. And dried plums, their pits replaced by whole walnuts, are enjoyed as snacks in the winter.[25]

Editor

Peach, Apricot, or Cherry Squares (Lepény)

Known as lepény *in Hungarian, this easy-to-make fruit-filled treat is a cross between the Hungarian* pite *(pie) and a soufflé, with a texture similar to French clafoutis. The mixture is baked in a rectangular pan and cut into squares for serving.*

Batter

6 large eggs
6 tablespoons granulated sugar
6 tablespoons all-purpose flour
½ teaspoon baking powder

Fruit

Use any *one* of these suggested fruits:
6 large peaches, peeled, cored, thinly sliced, and fanned out, sprinkled with lemon juice to preserve the color, OR
14 fresh apricots, prepared as above, OR
2 cups pitted sour or sweet cherries

Garnish

Confectioners' sugar

▶ Preheat the oven to 350°F. Butter a 9 × 13–inch rectangular baking pan and sprinkle it with flour, shaking off the excess.

▶ **Batter:** In the bowl of a stand mixer fitted with the whisk attachment, beat the eggs with sugar at high speed for about 10 minutes, until light and fluffy. They will resemble whipped cream.

- In a separate bowl, whisk together the flour and baking powder. Turn the mixer speed to low. Add the flour mixture to the eggs, 1 tablespoon at a time, to make a smooth batter.

▶ **Fruit:** Pour half of the batter into the baking pan. Place the fruit evenly on the top. Pour the remaining batter evenly over the fruit.

- Bake at 350°F on the middle rack of the oven for 35 to 40 minutes. Let the cake cool completely in the pan set on a wire rack. It will deflate slightly as it cools.

▶ **Garnish:** Sift confectioners' sugar over the top and cut into squares.

▶ Makes 20 servings.

OTHER HUNGARIAN HOMESTYLE DESSERTS

▶ **NOTE:** In these recipes, volume measurements of *nut flours* (in cups) are an approximation, to the nearest fraction of a cup, based on grinding the amount of *whole nuts* listed in the recipe. Volume measurements of nut flours can vary slightly, depending on the size of the nuts and the method used for grinding them. Since hand-ground nut flours are fluffier and less dense than store-bought nut flours, the volume of hand-ground nut flour can be slightly larger than the volume of store-bought nut flour, even though they both weigh the same. Likewise, tortes made with commercially ground nut flours tend to be a bit denser than those made with nuts ground by hand.

For best results measure out the amount of *whole nuts* needed in a recipe (in cups, or by weight in ounces), then grind them in your own kitchen and use the amount of nut flour that you produce. If using *store-bought nut flour*, then use the number of cups of *nut flour* specified in the recipe.

Hungarian Love Letters

This is my own easy-to-make adaptation of a traditional recipe from an heirloom recipe collection. Classic recipes often use a cream-cheese pastry, and the dough can be folded over the filling in several ways. They are called "love letters" because the sweet filling is hidden inside the pastry, like a love letter inside an envelope.

Dough

5 large egg yolks
⅓ cup granulated sugar
Pinch of salt
¾ stick (6 tablespoons, 3 ounces) unsalted butter, at room temperature
¼ cup half-and-half
2 cups all-purpose flour

Filling

1¼ cups walnuts (about 4½ ounces walnuts)
1 tablespoon granulated sugar
2 large egg whites
Pinch of salt
½ cup confectioners' sugar
Finely grated zest of 1 large lemon

Assembly

1 egg yolk
½ teaspoon water
1 egg white, lightly beaten

Garnish

Confectioners' sugar

▶ **Dough:** In the bowl of a stand mixer fitted with the paddle attachment, beat the egg yolks well with the sugar and salt. Add the butter and beat for 2 minutes longer. Add the half-and-half, mixing well. Add the flour,

½ cup at a time, and beat for an additional 3 minutes to make a firm dough. When ready, the dough will pull away from the sides of the bowl.

- Divide the dough in half. Place a large sheet of parchment paper on a work surface and dust it with flour. Put one of the dough halves on the parchment paper and place a second sheet of the same size parchment on top. Use a rolling pin to roll out the dough into a 9 × 9–inch square. Repeat with the remaining dough half. Wrap the two dough squares separately in plastic wrap or aluminum foil and refrigerate for 3 hours.

▶ **Filling:** Pulse the walnuts in a food processor with 1 tablespoon granulated sugar for only a few seconds, until they become powdered. Do not overprocess or the walnuts will turn into a paste.

- Use a small handheld mixer to beat the egg whites with a pinch of salt in a medium bowl to form stiff peaks. In another bowl whisk together the confectioners' sugar, lemon zest, and powdered walnuts. Fold this mixture into the egg whites. Cover and refrigerate.

▶ **Assembly:** Preheat the oven to 325°F. Line an 11 × 17–inch rimmed baking sheet with parchment paper. Make an egg wash by whisking together the egg yolk and ½ teaspoon water in a small bowl.

- Lightly beat the egg white in another small bowl. Place one 9 × 9–inch dough square on a work surface, and use a fluted-edge pastry cutter to cut it into nine smaller 3 × 3–inch squares. Repeat with the other dough square, cutting it into nine smaller squares.

- Place 1 teaspoon of the walnut filling in the center of each square. Brush the edges with the beaten egg white, and fold the squares into triangles, pressing to seal firmly. Place the triangles on the prepared baking sheet and brush the top of the pastries with the egg-yolk wash.

- Bake on the middle rack of the oven at 325°F for 25 minutes or until golden-brown in color. Remove the pastries from the pan and let them cool completely on a wire rack. Before serving, lightly sift confectioners' sugar over the top. Serve immediately or store in a cookie jar with parchment paper between each layer of pastries.

▶ Makes 18 pastries.

Sour Cherry-and-Walnut Squares

This delicious little treat is easy to make and features sour cherries, which are much loved in Hungary. It's also easy to carry to picnics or bake sales, instead of brownies or lemon bars.

Dough

1 stick (8 tablespoons, 4 ounces, ½ cup) unsalted butter, at room temperature
1 cup granulated sugar
2 large eggs
¾ cup milk
2 tablespoons pure vanilla extract
2 cups walnut flour (made from about 7 ounces or 2 cups of walnuts)
2 cups all-purpose flour
1 tablespoon baking powder

Fruit

1 pound fresh sour cherries, pitted and well drained (with the juice reserved), or one 24-ounce jar of pitted sour cherry compote, drained (with the juice reserved)

Sour-cherry syrup

Reserved cherry juice
½ cup granulated sugar

▶ Preheat the oven to 325°F. Butter the bottom and sides of a 9 × 13 × 2–inch baking pan. Sprinkle with flour and shake out the excess.

▶ **Dough:** In the bowl of a heavy-duty stand mixer fitted with the paddle attachment, beat the butter with the sugar for 3 minutes, or until light and fluffy. Add the eggs, milk, and vanilla and beat for 2 more minutes.

- In a separate bowl, mix together the walnut flour, all-purpose flour, and baking powder. Add this to the butter mixture, ½ cup at a time, mixing at medium speed until a smooth dough forms.

- Press the dough into the prepared pan. Arrange the sour cherries evenly on top of the dough. Bake on the middle rack of the oven at 325°F for 30 minutes. When the pastry is done, it should feel firm to the touch and be a light golden-brown color. Let it cool in the pan set on a wire rack.

▶ **Sour-cherry syrup:** Combine the reserved cherry juice with the sugar in a saucepan. Bring to a boil over medium heat, then simmer for 5 to 10 minutes, until the mixture begins to thicken. Set aside and let cool before serving.

- Cut the pastry into 2-inch squares. Dust the top with confectioners' sugar. Serve with a tablespoon of syrup drizzled over the top or pooled on the individual serving plates.

▶ Makes 24 squares.

Snow Balls (Sweet Dumplings)

This recipe is dedicated to my friend Szarka Józsefné, who graciously shared her family's own recipe with me. Snow Balls are a typical Hungarian dessert, a kind of sweet white dumpling that is very traditional in Central Europe. They bring back memories of my childhood, when they were often served in the afternoon when we returned home from school.

2 large eggs, at room temperature
11 ounces (weight) of dry farmers' cheese (pot cheese),* at room temperature, pressed through a sieve
7 tablespoons quick-cooking farina (Instant Cream of Wheat)
1 tablespoon granulated sugar
1 cup confectioners' sugar
¾ stick (6 tablespoons, 3 ounces) unsalted butter
1 cup plain fresh breadcrumbs
*Fresh white cheese, much firmer than American cottage cheese, which is available at most large supermarkets and delicatessens.

- Beat the eggs lightly with a fork in a medium bowl. Mash the farmers' cheese into the eggs, mixing well. Add the farina, granulated sugar, and confectioners' sugar, and continue mashing until all ingredients are well blended. Let the mixture rest for 20 minutes.

- Heat the butter in a skillet and fry the fresh breadcrumbs until they become light golden-brown in color.

- Fill a medium-large saucepan halfway with water and bring it to a simmer over medium heat. Using a tablespoon, scoop out a rounded mound of dough. Wet your hands with cold water and form the dough into a ball. Immediately drop the ball into the simmering water. Don't crowd the dumplings in the pan. Cook in batches for about 8 minutes after the water has come back to a simmer.

- Use a slotted spoon to lift the balls out of the water one at a time, letting them drain well. Then place them on top of the breadcrumbs in the skillet, and roll them around to coat the balls entirely with breadcrumbs.

- To serve, generously sprinkle the top with the confectioners' sugar. Pass extra confectioners' sugar for people who would like these a bit sweeter.

▶ Makes about 14 dumplings.

HUNGARIAN DUMPLINGS

Hungarians love dumplings, which they make in many different shapes, sizes, and flavors. Ingredients include flour, semolina, potatoes, cornmeal, day-old bread, eggs, and even minced meat or vegetables. Shapes range from free-form to round to long with pointed ends. Tiny flour-and-egg dumplings are cooked in soups and stews or tossed together with cheese for a filling main dish. Large savory dumplings are an accompaniment to many meat dishes, especially those with sauces for the dumplings to absorb. Sweet dumplings often have a whole fruit hiding in the center. Others are made from fresh white farmers' cheese and sugar, bound together with flour and eggs. Garnished with confectioners' sugar, sweet dumplings are eaten not only for dessert but also, in former times, as a main dish. And many Hungarian dumplings, both sweet and savory, are rolled in fried bread crumbs just before serving.

Editor

Hungarian Apple Pancakes

One of the defining differences between Hungarian pancakes and those from some other parts of the world is the addition of carbonated water, which makes these pancakes light and fluffy. This easy-to-make recipe produces very delicate, thin pancakes. They can be served for breakfast, as an afternoon snack, or for a light, family-style dessert.

Batter

3 large eggs
1 cup milk
2 tablespoons granulated sugar
¼ teaspoon salt
2 cups all-purpose flour
2 large Granny Smith apples, peeled
½ cup carbonated water
Unsalted butter, for cooking

Garnish

½ cup confectioners' sugar
1 teaspoon ground cinnamon
Apricot preserves (optional)

▶ **Batter:** Combine the eggs, milk, sugar, and salt in a large bowl. Using a handheld mixer, add the flour, blending together to make a smooth batter. Let rest at room temperature for 1 hour.

- Peel the apples. Using the largest holes on a box grater, grate enough apples to equal 2 cups. Just before cooking the pancakes, stir the carbonated water and grated apples into the batter.

- Heat a large frying pan or griddle. When the pan is hot, drop in about 1 tablespoon of butter and let it melt to cover the bottom of the pan. Pour ¼ cup of batter onto the pan and swirl it around to spread the batter out a bit. When one side is cooked (just lightly browned), flip the pancake over. Cook the other side until it is lightly browned. It is best to serve these pancakes immediately, but you can also stack them on a plate, cover them loosely with foil, and keep them warm in a 200°F oven.

▶ **Garnish:** Before serving, whisk together the confectioners' sugar and cinnamon in a small bowl. To serve, place one pancake on a plate, sprinkle it with the cinnamon sugar, and repeat until you have a stack of three. You can also serve some apricot preserves on the side.

▶ Makes 12 to 14 pancakes.

HUNGARIAN PANCAKES

Thin pancakes known as *palacsinta* (pah-la-CHIN-ta) are very popular in Hungary, where they are eaten in many forms, both savory and sweet, as appetizers, main dishes, and desserts. Made from a simple mixture of flour, eggs, salt, and milk—and a little sugar for sweet pancakes—the batter is usually lightened by the addition of carbonated water. But the great variety of Hungarian pancakes comes from their shapes, fillings, and garnishes, limited only by the cook's imagination.

Pancakes are sliced into strips for adding to soups, folded into triangles or rolled into cylinders around fillings, or stacked flat with fillings between them. Some are even folded into squares around a filling, dipped in beaten egg and bread crumbs, and then deep-fried. Others are rolled into cylinders around a filling, snuggled into a baking dish, and baked with custard or meringue on top.

Popular sweet fillings include ground almonds or walnuts, ground poppy seeds, sweetened chestnut puree, raisins, candied fruit peel, and a variety of fruit and berry preserves. Sweet pancakes are often served with a garnish of whipped cream, ice cream, confectioners' sugar, vanilla-scented granulated sugar, chocolate sauce, or a combination of these.

Editor

Cheese Biscuits (Pogácsa)

*Following tradition, I made a small hand-embroidered pouch to carry on my
high-school graduation day. On that day when we said good-bye to our alma
mater, we all dressed up in our navy-blue pleated skirts and white blouses
and carried our* utitáska *(travel bag), the little bag that each of us had made.
In the bag we carried a Hungarian coin and a* pogácsák, *(cheese biscuit)—
all we needed to start the journey of life: food and money. This custom still
continues today in my hometown of Hódmezővásárhely.*

Dough

1 package (¼ ounce) dry yeast
Pinch of sugar
¼ cup lukewarm whole milk (105–110°F)
2 pounds sifted all-purpose flour (about 8 cups)
4 sticks (32 tablespoons, 16 ounces, 2 cups) unsalted butter, at
  room temperature
1 tablespoon salt
3 large eggs, lightly beaten
¾ cup sour cream, at room temperature
¾ cup milk, at room temperature
2 cups coarsely grated Edam cheese
1 stick (8 tablespoons, 4 ounces, ½ cup) butter, melted (for
  brushing on the dough)
Caraway seeds (optional)

Egg wash

2 egg yolks
2 teaspoons of water

▶ Dough: In a small bowl whisk the yeast and sugar into the ¼ cup of
  warm milk. Cover and set aside for 10 minutes to let it bubble up.

  • In a larger bowl, whisk together the flour and salt, then gently work
    the butter into the flour with your hands, rubbing the ingredients
    together. (Or mix all these ingredients together in a food processor.)

- Stir the eggs, sour cream, and milk together in another bowl. Add this mixture, along with the yeast mixture, to the flour mixture. Knead well, making a soft dough. Add the grated cheese and knead to incorporate it into the dough. Form the dough into a ball. Wrap in plastic wrap and refrigerate for 30 minutes.

- Roll out the dough into a rectangular shape until about ¼- to ½–inch thick. Brush with melted butter, then fold into thirds. Roll out again to ¼- or ½–inch thick, brush with melted butter, and fold into thirds again. Brush with butter, and repeat folding one more time. Roll out once more and then fold in half. Tap with a rolling pin or press down with your hands to even out the dough.

- Wrap in plastic wrap and refrigerate for at least 1 hour or overnight. If chilled overnight, let the dough sit at room temperature for 15 to 30 minutes before continuing with the next step.

- Position an oven rack on the lower level of the oven. Preheat the oven to 350°F. Butter an 11 × 17–inch baking sheet.

- Roll out the dough to ½–inch thickness. Use a knife to score diagonal crisscrosses on the top. Cut the dough into rounds with 1½–inch round cookie or biscuit cutter and place the dough rounds on the baking sheet 2 inches apart.

▶ **Egg wash:** Whisk together the egg yolks and water in a small bowl. Use a pastry brush to brush the top of each biscuit with the egg wash. Sprinkle the tops with caraway seeds if desired.

- Bake the biscuits at 350°F for approximately 25 minutes on the lower rack of the oven, until golden-brown. Remove the biscuits from the pan and let them cool on a wire rack. When completely cool, store them in a tightly covered container.

▶ Makes 80 little cheese biscuits.

HUNGARIAN FLAKY BISCUITS
(POGÁCSA)

Hungarians love their *pogácsa* (poh-GAH-tcha), little round flaky pastries that could be described as a cross between American biscuits and British scones. Light and tender, they can be savory or sweet, are made in many flavors, and range in size from bite-size tiny to as large as your fist.

The basic dough—which might or might not include yeast—always contains plenty of fat: butter, lard, full-fat farmers' cheese, sour cream, shredded hard cheese. Pork or goose cracklings, or even finely shredded onions or cabbage fried in butter, can be kneaded into the dough, which is usually rolled out and folded over several times to make the flaky layers of a good *pogácsák*. After being cut into rounds with a pastry cutter, the top is often scored with a knife to make a crosshatch design or brushed with egg and sprinkled with sesame, caraway, poppy, or sunflower seeds, chopped garlic, shredded cheese, black pepper, or paprika before baking.

Pogácsa are eaten throughout the day, at breakfast, for a snack, as an appetizer, and at dinner. Corner bakeries and small bake shops in subway stations sell *pogácsa* to Hungarians on the go. Small *pogácsa* are served as finger food to accompany predinner drinks. And some restaurants include a basket of *pogácsa*, wrapped in a napkin to keep warm, with your order for a meal. But whatever time of day or night, *pogácsa* are always best eaten hot from the oven.

Editor

Walnut or Poppy-Seed Pastry Rolls (Beigli)

In Hungarian households, a few days before Christmas a turkey is purchased and the traditional walnut or poppy-seed beigli *are baked. No Hungarian Christmas would be complete without* beigli. *We bake these as a family activity, freeze them, and ship them across the country to our family and friends to enjoy during the holidays. Now you can start your own holiday tradition by making these delicious rolled-and-filled, log-shaped pastries yourself.*

▶ **NOTE:** This recipe is for *beigli* with a walnut filling. If you want to make them with a poppy-seed filling, see the variation at the end of this recipe. If you want to make four *beigli*—two with walnut filling and two with poppy seeds—use the main recipe for the dough and a half recipe of each of the two fillings.

Dough

4 sticks (32 tablespoons, 16 ounces, 2 cups) unsalted butter, cut into ½-inch cubes, at room temperature
2 pounds unbleached all-purpose flour (about 8 cups)
1 teaspoon yeast
¼ cup lukewarm milk (105–115°F)
3 large eggs, at room temperature
½ cup sour cream, at room temperature
¼ cup milk, at room temperature
3 tablespoons sugar
2 rounded teaspoons salt

Filling

14 cups walnut flour (firmly packed, made from about 3 pounds of walnuts)
2 cups milk
2 cups granulated sugar
Finely grated zest of 4 lemons
1 (15-ounce) box of golden raisins
3 egg whites, stiffly beaten

Egg wash

3 egg yolks
1 tablespoon water

Garnish

Confectioners' sugar

▶ **Dough:** In a large bowl combine the butter and the flour, mixing with your fingers or a pastry blender, until it resembles coarse breadcrumbs.

● Dissolve the yeast in ¼ cup of lukewarm milk in a small bowl. In a 2-cup glass measuring cup, lightly whisk together the eggs, sour cream, ¼ cup of room-temperature milk, sugar, and salt. This should total 2 cups of liquid; if it does not, add more milk to make 2 cups. Stir the dissolved yeast into this mixture.

● Add the yeast mixture to the butter-flour mixture. Knead it well with the heel of your palm until firm and smooth. Cover the bowl with a tea towel and let the dough rest for 2 hours.

● Form the dough into four large equal-size balls, plus one small ball for decoration. Flatten each ball a little into a disk.

▶ **Filling:** Bring the milk and the sugar to a boil in a large saucepan, stirring to dissolve the sugar. Pour the walnut flour into the milk and mix well. Remove the pan from the heat. The mixture will look mushy. Stir in the lemon zest and the raisins, then let cool completely. Fold in the stiffly beaten egg whites. Divide the filling into four equal proportions.

▶ Preheat the oven to 350°F. Butter two 11 × 17–inch rimmed baking sheets, line them with parchment paper, and butter the parchment paper. In a small bowl, whisk together the egg yolks and water.

▶ **Assembly:** Lightly flour a work surface. Roll out one of the four disks into a 9 × 12–inch rectangle. Spread one-fourth of the filling evenly on the dough. Starting with the long side of the dough, roll it into a log, like a jelly roll. Pinch the ends closed.

- Place on the prepared baking pan. You can bake two *beigli* on one pan. Immediately brush the top with the egg wash. Repeat with the other three portions of dough and filling. Allow the *beigli* to rest for 20 minutes.

▶ **Decorations:** To decorate the top of the *beigli*, roll out the reserved small disk of dough. With a small cookie cutter, cut out some hearts or other desired shapes. Dip the cut-out dough into the egg wash and arrange a few on the top of *beigli*. Pierce the sides and top of the dough in several places with a skewer or fork so the steam can escape during baking.

- Bake the *beigli* on the middle rack of the oven at 350°F for 30 minutes, or until deep golden brown. If longer baking is needed, reduce temperature to 325°F. Let the *beigli* cool completely on a wire rack.

▶ **Garnish:** Sift confectioners' sugar over the top. To serve, cut crosswise into slices.

Hungarians cooks often bake several *beigli* for the Christmas season.

▶ Makes four logs. Each log makes 12 slices.

Alternative poppy-seed filling

▶ NOTE: Ground poppy seeds can be purchased at specialty food shops and online.

3 cups milk
1¾ cups granulated sugar
6½ cups (2 pounds) ground poppy seeds
Finely grated zest of 3 large lemons
1 cup golden raisins (6 ounces)

- Bring the milk and the sugar to a boil in a large saucepan. Stir in the ground poppy seeds and cook for 10 minutes over low heat, stirring constantly. Let cool. Stir in the lemon zest and raisins. Use this filling instead of the walnut filling in the *beigli* recipe.

Two kinds of Hungarian *beigli*, yeast-raised roulades with walnut and poppyseed fillings.

HUNGARIAN *BEIGLI*

Beigli (BAY-glee) are Hungarian roulades made with a yeast dough rolled out very thin, spread with a sweet filling, rolled up, and brushed with beaten egg before baking. Traditional for Christmas, they can be bought at bakeries, but homemade are always considered superior. Home cooks compete with their relatives and friends to bake the best *beigli* during the Christmas season—often resulting in a glut of *beigli* at this time of year, giving rise to *beigli* jokes like fruitcake jokes in America.

The yeast dough is enriched with plenty of butter and sometimes sour cream, too, although in earlier times *beigli* were often made with lard instead of butter. The two traditional fillings are finely ground nuts (walnuts, hazelnuts, or almonds) and ground poppy seeds—sweetened with sugar, honey, or fruit jam, and often enhanced with cinnamon and other spices, lemon or orange zest, cake or bread crumbs, candied fruit peel, and raisins, sultanas, or dried currants. The roulade is brushed with beaten egg (sometimes in a two-step process with the yolk and white separated), which is allowed to dry before baking, to produce the *beigli*'s characteristic mahogany-brown crust with a crackled surface.

Some bakeries now sell *beigli* made with fillings of sweetened chestnut puree or chocolate, but purists insist on fillings of poppy seeds (symbols of prosperity and fertility) and walnuts (said to keep trouble at bay).

Editor

HUNGARIAN CHRISTMAS TRADITIONS

In Hungary the Christmas season begins on December 6, known as the Saint Nicholas Feast Day or the birthday of Szent Mikulás, the Hungarian version of Saint Nicholas, or Santa Claus. The night before, the children shine their shoes and place them on the windowsill, awaiting treats brought by Szent Mikulás.

When the children are asleep, their parents fill the little shoes with a red cellophane bag full of shelled walnuts, peanuts, various hard candies, chocolates, and maybe a treasured orange. If a child has been naughty, there will be a twig sticking out of his or her shoe. In the morning, full of excitement, we couldn't wait to run into the room and find the shiny red bags filling our own shoes. I don't have to tell you how much candy was consumed on that morning. Even today this custom is celebrated the same way in Hungary.

At Christmastime even the most modest households display apples and walnuts on their table. Christmas Eve is known as Szent-este, Holy Evening. Children hide a walnut shell for the angels and little Jesus (Jézuska), who bring the Christmas tree and presents. The parents have already decorated the Christmas tree secretly, usually when the children are out of the house. I remember as a child the marvelous element of surprise when, after dinner was finished, we could hear the little angel's bells ring, signaling that it was time to open the living room door, revealing the fully lit Christmas tree festooned with *szaloncukor*, pieces of fondant or chocolate filled with marzipan and wrapped in glittering multi-colored foil. What a lovely sight! And of course there were always gifts under the tree, too.

Ella Szabó

ACKNOWLEDGMENTS

As I write these acknowledgments posthumously for my dear mother, Ella Kovács Szabó, I am grateful and overwhelmed by the gracious, selfless support and encouragement by so many people, over several decades, who have helped bring this book to fruition. This has been a multifamily, multi-generational endeavor, guided by a shared love of Hungarian pastries, love for one another, and the fulfillment of promises made.

Without question I offer my greatest thanks to Isabella Eckmayer, known to me as Belli Tante, who gave my mother her treasured personal Hungarian pastry recipes from the Belle Époque—the period from the late nineteenth century up to World War I—which became the inspiration for this book. Over the years her daughter, Judith Eckmayer-Wedow, who was my mother's best friend, and Judith's daughter, Julie Wedow–von Kreutzbruck, my own best friend, have contributed invaluable support and intimate knowledge pertaining to the stories and recipes in this book. Thank goodness Julie safeguarded the original handwritten recipes that now appear in this book. She helped write the history of those recipes' journey, too.

Fate extended a gentle hand and brought the generous and amazing author and editor Sharon Hudgins into my life. Sharon had consulted with my mother and father about this book more than fifteen years ago and encouraged them to pursue writing it. I can honestly say that I would never have been able to complete this project without Sharon's help, and I offer my profound thanks and gratitude to her.

There are a number of other professional editors, chefs, and authors who also consulted and provided support to Mom, including the legendary Julia Child, whose seismic impact on the culinary world continues even today. We met Julia on her 90th birthday, and when she learned of Mother's book, she wholeheartedly encouraged her to get it published.

The highly accomplished chef and author Rick Rodgers had a very special relationship with my parents and encouraged Mom to carry on with her manuscript. He also asked her to consult on his own book *Kaffeehaus: Exquisite Desserts from Classic Cafés of Vienna, Budapest, and Prague,* to vet the Hungarian recipes in it. (One of Mom's recipes for walnut tortes appears in his book.) Serendipity brought Rick and me together many years later. I am grateful for his guidance and support; it was an experience of friendship truly coming full circle.

In addition, Susan Derecsky, author of *The Hungarian Cookbook,* and Karen Berman, a writer and editor who specialized in food and lifestyle topics, graciously lent their support to my mother and helped her with this book.

Numerous family members and dear friends also helped over the decades, especially with the taste-testing of all those tortes and pastries! My father was a lucky and very willing "super taster," since Mom was baking all the time. Later my family became the happy recipients of her kitchen endeavors, with my husband Russell and our sons, Russell and Spencer, cheering on her work and asking their grandmother, Nana, to bring tortes and cookies whenever she came to visit. Nana joyfully engaged the boys in nut grinding and baking projects when she stayed with us, and the boys still continue to help with the baking whenever they're home for a visit. The continued encouragement and support from mom's dear girlfriends cannot go unnoted, including Elizabeth Antal, her friend since kindergarten, and these other dear women: Agnés Czirják, Maria Tomasz, Olga Kaali, and Doris Jacobson.

This book has been a family effort for many decades, with everyone helping in some way, but Dad did the lion's share of taste-testing, as well as typing and organizing recipes and photographing many of the results. My cousin Agnés Kovács-Blonnigen has been of invaluable help during this past year, translating my grandmother's recipes from Hungarian and answering other Hungarian-related questions.

Sally Gundy, Mother's friend from the days when they taught together in New York City, helped in the laborious translation of Belli Tante's recipes from German. The Countess Éva Edelsheim Gyulai also helped in this task. Her son Peter Kendeffy and his family were frequently at our home and happily taste-tested many of the tortes; his first wife Magdalena's summer fruit recipe provided inspiration for another recipe in this book. Other family friends contributed recipes, including Judith Schultze's delicious version of Gerbeaud pastry. Dee Lewis, family friend and caterer, helped bake, organize, and refine many recipes. Julie Tomasz graciously offered to translate

Mom's story "Of Hunger and Oranges" from the original Hungarian, keeping Mom's voice distinct in that poignant piece.

Although I write these acknowledgments posthumously for my mother, I am compelled to recognize and thank her for having lovingly nurtured this cookbook over several decades. I am honored to have had the opportunity to memorialize her life's work. She joyfully embraced the challenge from Belli Tante to bring these historical recipes to you, the reader, and it became her passion project; her tenacity and dedication is inspiring, like her life's journey. All of us involved enjoyed the fruits of her labor and happily contributed as best we could, and we all are better for it. She baked into this book her love for her mother country's history and gastronomic and cultural delights, her love of baking, and her sincere desire to share her joyful passion with you.

As for me and my efforts on this creative journey, where would I be without the love, support, and encouragement of my dear family and amazing friends who heartened and cheered me on? For their help, from more testing and tasting to helping with research and translations to emboldening me to bake the recipes and take photos, I offer my heartfelt thanks.

Lastly, I offer my thanks and gratitude to the University of North Texas press for seeing the intrinsic value in preserving and publishing these updated historical Hungarian torte and dessert recipes as Number 6 in the Great American Cooking Series. It has been an absolute pleasure working collaboratively with Director Ron Chrisman and Managing Editor Amy Maddox. As I am a novice in the publishing world, they patiently explained and professionally guided me through all of the steps to bring this delicious project to fruition.

As they have for multiple generations in both Europe and America, may these recipes bring you happiness in their preparation in your own kitchen and be shared joyfully with your family and special friends.

Eve Aino Roza Wirth

2023

ENDNOTES

1. Anikó Gergely, *Culinaria Hungary* (English edition) (Cologne: Könemann Verlagsgesellschaft GmbH, 1999), 158–63; Darra Goldstein, ed., *The Oxford Companion to Sugar and Sweets* (Oxford: Oxford University Press, 2015), 35–39, 769–71; Rick Rodgers, *Kaffeehaus: Exquisite Desserts from Classic Cafés of Vienna, Budapest, and Prague* (New York: Clarkson Potter, 2002), 51, 114–15.

2. Wikipedia, "Crvenka," last modified October 16, 2022, 19:12, https://en.wikipedia.org/wiki/Crvenka; Wikipedia, "Yugoslavia," last modified on August 20, 2023, 14:33, https://en.wikipedia.org/wiki/Yugoslavia.

3. Gergely, *Culinaria Hungary*, 184–87; EU Fruit And Vegetables Market Observatory, Pip Fruit Subgroup, *The Apple Market in the EU: Vol. 1: Production, Areas And Yields*, September 26, 2022, https://agriculture.ec.europa.eu/system/files/2022-10/apples-production_en.pdf; "Around the World—Hungary," *Ambrosia Apples*, accessed September 7, 2023, https://ambrosiaapples.ca/around-the-world-hungary.

4. Gergely, *Culinaria Hungary*, 277; Rodgers, *Kaffeehaus*, 130–31.

5. E. Kállay and G. Szenci, "Cherry Production in Hungary," *International Society for Horticultural Science*, accessed September 7, 2023, https://www.ishs.org/ishs-article/410_40.

6. Gergely, *Culinaria Hungary*, 232–33.

7. Gergely, *Culinaria Hungary*, 170; Sharon Hudgins, "Magnificent Marzipan," *European Traveler*, accessed September 7, 2023, https://europeantraveler.net/2022/05/03/magnificent-marzipan; Ella Kovács Szabó, "All About Almonds," *Greenwich* [Connecticut] *Time*, May 2, 2001, section B, 1–2.

8. "Hazelnut Production by Country 2023," *World Population Review*, accessed September 7, 2023, https://worldpopulationreview.com/country-rankings/hazelnut-production-by-country.

9. Ella Kovács Szabó, "All about Hazelnuts!" *Greenwich* [Connecticut] *Time*, January 16, 2002, section B, 1–2.

10. Imperial Torte Vienna (website), accessed September 7, 2023, https://www.imperialtorte.com/en/.

11. Geza Bujdosó, "The Hungarian Shell Fruit Industry: Actual Situation, Possibilities in the Future," (paper presented at NARIC Fruitculture Research Institute, Budapest, Hungary, November 10–11, 2015), https://researchgate.net/publication/285120488; Gergely, *Culinaria Hungary*, 201; Goldstein, *Oxford Companion to Sugar and Sweets*, 489.

12. Ella Kovács Szabó, "Wonderful World of Walnuts," *Greenwich* [Connecticut] *Time*, May 15, 2002, section C, 1–2.

13. Bujdosó, "Hungarian Shell Fruit Industry"; Gergely, *Culinaria Hungary*, 281–83; "How Chestnut Purée Became Part of the Traditional Christmas Menu," *Liszt Institute, Hungarian Cultural Center New York*, December 15, 2021, https://culture.hu/us/new-york/articles/how-chestnut-puree-became-part-of-the-traditional-christmas-menu.

14. Goldstein, *Oxford Companion to Sugar and Sweets*, 405–6; Rodgers, *Kaffeehaus*, 54.

15. Gergely, *Culinaria Hungary*, 179; Alexandra Czeglédi and Gosztonyi Balazs, "Falling into Pieces by the Drupelets: The Collapse of the Hungarian Raspberry Production" (paper presented at 16th Biennial Conference of European Association of Social Anthropologists: New Anthropological Horizons in and beyond Europe, University of Lisbon [virtual], Lisbon, Portugal, July 20–24, 2020), https://nomadit.co.uk/conference/easa2020/paper/54406.

16. Wikipedia, "Siege of Sevastopol," last modified on September 9, 2023, 18:00, https://en.wikipedia.org/wiki/Siege_of_Sevastopol_(1854%E2%80%931855).

17. Albert Shumate, "An Early Attempt at International Goodwill," *California Historical Quarterly* 50, no. 1 (1971): 79–83.

18. George Lang, *The Cuisine of Hungary* (New York: Bonanza Books, 1971), 408–9.

19. Rodgers, *Kaffeehaus*, 50, 54.

20. Goldstein, *Oxford Companion to Sugar and Sweets*, 36.

21. Gergely, *Culinaria Hungary*, 110–13; D. Surányi, "Apricot Culture in Hungary: Past And Present" (paper presented at International

Symposium on Apricot Culture, Veria-Makedonia, Greece, May 25–30, 1997), https://www.actahort.org/books/488/488_30.htm.

22. Gergely, *Culinaria Hungary*, 160–61; "Gerbeaud Legend," *Café Gerbeaud, Budapest*, accessed September 7, 2023, https://gerbeaud.hu/en/legend/.

23. Goldstein, *Oxford Companion to Sugar and Sweets*, 311–13; Sharon Hudgins, "Alsatian Kugelhopf: A Cake for All Seasons," *Gastronomica: The Journal of Food and Culture* 10, no. 4 (2010): 62–66.

24. Anna Wynn, "Recipe of the Week: Russian Cream Cake," *Daily News Hungary*, May 23, 2018, https://dailynewshungary.com/recipe-of-the-week-russian-cream-cake/.

25. Gergely, *Culinaria Hungary*, 188–93, 196–97; Elek Magyar, *The Gourmet's Cookbook*, translated by Caroline Bodóczky, Judith Elliott, and Inez Kemenes, 2nd ed. (Budapest: Corvina, 1989), 574; L. Z. Kiss, "The Hungarian Plum Production and Export in the EU" (paper presented at 15th International Symposium on Horticultural Economics and Management, Berlin, Germany, August 29–September 3, 2004), https://doi.org/10.17660/ActaHortic.2004.655.46.

BIBLIOGRAPHY

Bennett, Paul Pogany, and Velma R. Clark. *The Art of Hungarian Cooking: Two Hundred and Twenty-Two Favorite Recipes*. New York: Hippocrene Books, 1997.

Bujdosó, Geza. "The Hungarian Shell Fruit Industry: Actual Situation, Possibilities in the Future." Paper presented at NARIC Fruitculture Research Institute, Budapest, Hungary, November 10–11, 2015. https://researchgate.net/publication/285120488.

Czeglédi, Alexandra, and Gosztonyi Balazs. "Falling into Pieces by the Drupelets: The Collapse of the Hungarian Raspberry Production." Paper presented at 16th Biennial Conference of European Association of Social Anthropologists: New Anthropological Horizons in and beyond Europe, University of Lisbon [virtual], Lisbon, Portugal, July 20–24, 2020. https://nomadit.co.uk/conference/easa2020/paper/54406.

Davidson, Alan. *The Oxford Companion to Food*. Oxford: Oxford University Press, 1999.

Derecskey, Susan. *The Hungarian Cookbook*. New York: Harper & Row, 1972.

Gergely, Anikó. *Culinaria Hungary*. English ed. Cologne: Könemann Verlagsgesellschaft GmbH, 1999.

Goldstein, Darra, ed. *The Oxford Companion to Sugar and Sweets*. Oxford: Oxford University Press, 2015.

Hajková, Mária. *Édeskönyv* [Book of Sweets]. Pozsony: Madách Publishing House, 1978.

Halász, Zoltán, and George Lang. *Gundel, 1894–1994*. Budapest: Helikon, 1993.

Hudgins, Sharon. "Alsatian Kugelhopf: A Cake for All Seasons." *Gastronomica: The Journal of Food and Culture* 10, no. 4 (2010): 62–66.

Hudgins, Sharon. "Magnificent Marzipan," *European Traveler*, accessed September 7, 2023, https://europeantraveler.net/2022/05/03/magnificent-marzipan.

228

Kálmán, Kalla, György Láng, and Zoltán Halász. *Gundel: ÚJ magyar szakácskönyv* [Gundel: The New Hungarian Cookbook]. Budapest: Pallas Stúdió, 1997.

Ketter, László. *Gasztronómiánk Krónikája: A Magyar Konyha Múltja És Jövője* [Chronicle of Our Gastronomy: The Past and Future of Hungarian Cuisine]. Budapest: Mezőgazdasági Kiadó, 1985.

Kiss, L. Z. "The Hungarian Plum Production and Export in the EU." Paper presented at 15th International Symposium on Horticultural Economics and Management, Berlin, Germany, August 29–September 3, 2004. https://doi.org/10.17660/ActaHortic.2004.655.46.

Lang, George. *The Cuisine of Hungary*. New York: Bonanza Books, 1971.

Magyar, Elek. *The Gourmet's Cookbook*. Translated by Caroline Bodóczky, Judith Elliott, and Inez Kemenes. 2nd ed. Budapest: Corvina, 1989.

Radke, Linda. F. *That Hungarian's in My Kitchen: 125 Hungarian American Kosher Recipes*. Chandler, AZ: Five Star Publications, 1997.

Rodgers, Rick. *Kaffeehaus: Exquisite Desserts from Classic Cafés of Vienna, Budapest, and Prague*. New York: Clarkson Potter, 2002.

Shumate, Albert. "An Early Attempt at International Goodwill." *California Historical Quarterly* 50, no. 1 (1971): 79–83.

Surányi, D. "Apricot Culture in Hungary: Past And Present." Paper presented at International Symposium on Apricot Culture, Veria-Makedonia, Greece, May 25–30, 1997. https://www.actahort.org/books/488/488_30.htm.

Szabó, Ella Kovács. "All about Almonds." *Greenwich* [Connecticut] *Time*. May 2, 2001, section B, 1–2.

Szabó, Ella Kovács. "All about Hazelnuts!" *Greenwich* [Connecticut] *Time*. January 16, 2002, section B, 1–2.

Szabó, Ella Kovács. "Wonderful World of Walnuts." *Greenwich* [Connecticut] *Time*. May 15, 2002, section C, 1–2.

Szathmáry, Louis. *The Bakery Restaurant Cookbook*. Boston: CBI, 1981.

Váncza, József. *A Mi Süteményes-könyvünk* [Our Cake Book]. Budapest: Váncza and Társa Food and Chemical Factory, 1936.

Venesz, József. *Hungarian Cuisine*. English ed. Budapest: Corvina Press, 1982.

Vizvári, Mariska. *Treasure Trove of Hungarian Cookery*. 4th rev. ed. Budapest: Corvina Kiadó, 1981.

Wynn, Anna. "Recipe of the Week: Russian Cream Cake." *Daily News Hungary*, May 23, 2018, https://dailynewshungary.com/recipe-of-the-week-russian-cream-cake/.

PHOTO CREDITS

Arto O. Szabó, pgs. xi, 9, 42, 138, 142, 161, 165, and in the center gallery, "Caramelized Hazelnut Torte with Chocolate Glaze," "Chocolate-Almond Torte with Apricot Glaze," "Cherry Sponge Cake," and "Hungarian Cheese Biscuits (*Pogácsa*)."

Eve Aino Roza Wirth, pgs. 13, 25, 27, 33, 34, 103, 107, 109, 127, 128, 153, 157, 182, 214, and in the center gallery, "Slice of King's Torte," "The King's Torte," "Judith's Recovery Torte,'" "Belli Tante's Apple Torte," "Caramelized-Almond Cream Torte," "Coffee-Almond Torte," "Almond-Flour Cake with Mixed Fruits," and "Loaves of *Beigli*."

Hu Totya, Wikimedia Creative Commons 4.0, pg. 215.

Illustratedjc, Wikimedia Commons 3.0, in the center gallery, "Gerbeaud Slice at Café Gerbeaud in Budapest."

Avi Deror, Wikimedia Commons, in the center gallery, "Classic Esterházy Torte at a coffeehouse/café in Vienna."

Bedinek, Wikimedia Creative Commons 4.0, in the center gallery, "Vanilla Crescent Cookies."

INDEX

Note: Page numbers in *italics* denote black-and-white images and associated captions. The page locator *"color gallery"* refers to the image gallery between pages 148 and 149.

ABOUT

Author

Ella Kovács Szabó (1929–2009) was born in Hungary and emigrated to the United States after the Hungarian Revolution of 1956. An avid sportswoman, she was a professional physical education instructor and a member of the 1960 US Olympic Synchronized Swimming Exhibition Team. She was also a talented baker who enjoyed sharing her culinary skills and delicious desserts with family, friends, readers, radio audiences, and many charities in New York and Connecticut.

Editor

Sharon Hudgins is an award-winning author, editor, journalist, and culinary historian who has traveled extensively in Hungary. Her books include *T-Bone Whacks and Caviar Snacks: Cooking with Two Texans in Siberia and the Russian Far East* (author) and *Food on the Move: Dining on the Legendary Railway Journeys of the World* (editor and contributing writer). She lived in Europe for 18 years and has been a National Geographic Expert on Danube River tours to Hungary, Austria, Slovakia, Germany, and the Czech Republic.

Contributor

Eve Aino Roza Wirth (daughter of Ella Kovács Szabó) grew up cooking and baking beside her mother, immersed in Hungarian customs and traditions. A graduate of the Rhode Island School of Design, her years have been spent as a graphic designer, event planner, fundraiser, nonprofit board member, mother, and wife.